Where Is God Not?

Where Is God Not?

An American Surgeon in India

Forrest C. Eggleston

PROVIDENCE HOUSE PUBLISHERS
Franklin, Tennessee

Printed in the United States of America

03   02   01   00   99   1   2   3   4   5

Library of Congress Catalog Card Number: 98-68653

ISBN: 1-57736-138-5

Cover design by Gary Bozeman

*All profits from this book will be used for
the benefit of medical mission work in the
developing world.*

PROVIDENCE HOUSE PUBLISHERS
238 Seaboard Lane • Franklin, Tennessee 37067
800-321-5692

For Barbara

and

Carol and Robert

Contents

Foreword

Dr. Forrest C. Eggleston has written a fascinating and inspirational book, *Where Is God Not? An American Surgeon in India*. It is the story of the faithful missionary service of Dr. Eggleston and his wife, Barbara, over thirty-three years in India. Even more importantly, it is the story of God's work through their lives and through the lives of their colleagues in Christ's service. Reading this book has been a blessing for me, and I am confident it will be for you as well.

As you will soon discover, the title, *Where Is God Not?*, is a quote from the earliest American Presbyterian missionary to the Punjab, Rev. John Lowrie. Arriving in Ludhiana in 1834 after a grueling journey in which his wife and missionary companions died, he encountered Maharajah Ranjit Singh, the leader of the empire of the Sikhs. The maharajah asked Lowrie, "Where is God?" To that inquiry Lowrie pointed to an important Christian truth when he responded with another insightful question, "Where is God not?" This book makes it very clear that God, who is omnipresent, has indeed been present in the Punjab region of India over the last half century.

Through wonderful real life stories Eggleston gives us a marvelous window on thirty-three years of life in the Punjab. It begins in 1953 when Forrest and Barbara Eggleston and their two children find themselves in a "strange new world," in Jubar,

India. There they begin their missionary service in a small sana-torium for those suffering from tuberculosis. We follow their lives for the next thirty-three years, both in Jubar and then at the Ludhiana Christian Medical College and Hospital, which has developed into one of the premier Christian medical institutions in the world today.

We learn of the life of people from all walks of life in India during most of its post-independence history. We experience the blessing of people being healed by dedicated Christian medical workers. We rejoice as we come to know through the printed page the joys of medical students learning the skills and gifts of healing. We get a sense of the transformation of a nation. Most of all, we celebrate the many indications of the work of the Holy Spirit in the lives of people who for most of us are literally on the other side of the world.

There are many books on the theology of mission, on Christian medical work, and on the politics, society, and religion of India. There are fresh insights into all of these areas in *Where Is God Not?* However, what makes this book so refreshing is that these concerns are not addressed in an abstract or theoretical way but rather through how they come alive in the lives of real people.

This is also a book about transitions and transformations:

- the transitions between India just after independence and India today,
- the transition of Ludhiana Christian Hospital from a small, struggling mission hospital to a leading center for the training of Christian doctors and nurses and a leading medical center,
- the transition in the leadership of mission work in India from missionaries to competent and effective Indian Christians, and
- the transformation of thousands of people whose lives have been healed in body and spirit by the faithful Christian people and institutions highlighted in this book.

It was my honor and privilege for over sixteen years to serve as the senior staff executive for the world mission program of the

Presbyterian Church (U.S.A.). During that time I experienced over and over again situations like those so well described by Eggleston. All over the world there are wonderful examples of how seeds that were faithfully planted by missionaries are being nurtured by Christians from all nations and are bearing fruit beyond our wildest imagination. That is certainly the case at Ludhiana Christian Medical College and Hospital, and we all owe a debt of gratitude to faithful servants of Christ like Barbara and Forrest Eggleston who have been used so well by God in this process.

In one of the later chapters in the book Dr. Eggleston describes his personal and deeply spiritual struggle in responding to the urgent requests of his colleagues to become the director at Ludhiana. He had been deeply committed to encouraging Indian leadership at the institution, and he knew that the Punjab was facing severe crises with the growing conflicts among its people. What led him to say "yes" to the call of his colleagues was the clear conviction that "We are not alone!" Forrest Eggleston knew then, as he had experienced many times before, that it is God that gives us the strength to do the work to which God calls us.

In many ways this book is an important reminder to all of us that "We are not alone!" It is certainly a reminder that we are not alone when we engage in Christian mission. *Where Is God Not?* is a ringing tribute to God's work through Presbyterian world mission, through our missionaries, and through our Christian partners in India. This is a true story of how against all odds God's grace and mercy enable faithful Christians to do things that would never be possible without the strength of a power beyond ourselves.

Once I started reading these exciting memoirs, it was not easy to put them down. I am confident that you will find *Where Is God Not?* to be as interesting, enjoyable, and inspirational as I have.

Clifton Kirkpatrick
Stated Clerk of the General Assembly
Presbyterian Church (U.S.A.)
September 12, 1998

Preface and Acknowledgments

It was a bright and sunny December afternoon in 1953 when the SS *Steel Age* noisily dropped anchor in Bombay (now Mumbai) harbor. After five long weeks we had finally reached India.

When Barbara and I and our two children debarked in December 1953, India was but six and a half years a free country still recovering from its long struggle for independence. The freedom movement had been mostly nonviolent, thanks to the genius of Mahatma Gandhi. Tragically, the partition of the land into an independent India and the new nation of Pakistan had been followed by communal rioting from which neither country had yet recovered.

Like most Americans, we knew shamefully little about India except that it was poor and crowded, with a sixth of the world's people living on but a fortieth of the world's land. Indians, as soon became apparent, were equally ignorant of the United States, and assumed that all Americans were rich.

Indians spoke sixteen major languages and hundreds of dialects. English was spoken by only a small minority scattered throughout the country. Eighty percent of the people professed to be Hindu, while 11 percent were Muslim, making India the third largest Muslim population in the world. Christians made up but 2.6 percent of the people closely followed by the Sikhs with 2 percent and small minorities of Parses, Jews, animists, and adherents of a wide variety of cults. Most of these minorities lived in enclaves of varying sizes which provided common support and protection.

We had been sent to run a small tuberculosis sanatorium affiliated with the Christian Medical College at Ludhiana. The Lady Irwin Tuberculosis Sanatorium at Jubar (named in honor of the wife of a former British viceroy) was perched on a mountain ridge in the second tier of the Himalayan mountains, some five thousand feet above sea level.

Our first year was spent at Jubar in mountains we quickly came to love. Unfortunately, the need for better surgical facilities made it necessary for us to move one hundred miles to the west, to the Christian Medical College at Ludhiana on the sweltering plains of Punjab State. However, we continued to run the sanatorium for the next nineteen years, visiting it every two to three weeks until it finally had to close, the victim of the changing pattern of tuberculosis care.

As a result, we were privileged to know and work with the friendly but poor and backward mountain people as well as their more sophisticated and richer cousins on the plains.

We survived floods and three wars, two with Pakistan (1965 and 1971) and one with China (1962), witnessed the "Green Revolution," and lived through years of civil unrest. Punjab State changed from a dusty, sandy desert to the breadbasket of India, with lush green fields laden with harvest, the envy of farmers everywhere. Health services improved and schools and colleges multiplied, offering hope for the future. Tragically, the mountain people benefited but little, and remained poor and impoverished.

When we sailed for India, we understood that I was to run the sanatorium and develop a program in chest surgery at the medical college. Shortly after moving to Ludhiana, I was asked to organize and run the department of general surgery at the medical college. The unexpected opportunity given at the young age of thirty-five to build and develop an academic department was both satisfying and professionally challenging. This was to occupy me fully for the next twenty-eight years, but was rewarding beyond belief.

During our last four years (1982–86) I served as the director of the institution and, as such, learned about the vagaries of administration and soon developed a new respect and sympathy for professional administrators.

It was an experience worth having—we learned patience, tolerance, and, most importantly, grew in faith.

Where necessary, names have been changed to safeguard the privacy of those concerned.

This book is the result of friends encouraging me to tell some of the experiences, joys, and frustrations my wife and I shared as medical missionaries in India.

I would like to thank Mr. Jonathan Graf, who reviewed this work and made excellent suggestions that have been incorporated into the writing. He encouraged me much more than he realized. Mrs. Elsie Langstrom, Mrs. Jill Meyers, Rev. Robert Abrams, and Mr. Robert Beard have also made useful suggestions. My wife has helped in proofreading and editing and also gave useful advice. However, all faults are my own.

Barbara and I want to thank the Presbyterian Church (U.S.A.) for their generous and prayerful support through many difficulties, both professional and personal, during our years abroad. In addition, we want to note with gratitude the equally generous support we received from the United Methodist Church during our first three years in India.

Regrettably, we shall never have an opportunity to thank the thousands of people, most of whom we have never met, who supported us and our endeavors through their tithes and gifts and love and prayers.

They made our work possible, for we truly went to India as their representatives.

PART ONE
JUBAR, INDIA

CHAPTER 1

The Road to India

DR. DANIEL LAI* LED ME THROUGH A MAZE OF CROWDED narrow back alleys to an enormous pile of rotting garbage at the edge of Kaiochow Bay, China. The mound was growing steadily as trucks and carts dumped refuse into the sea, slowly claiming new land from it. On one side of the stinking heap, women—some accompanied by young children—were picking through it, searching for bottle caps or anything else they could sell for a few cents.

A young man came toward us carrying a package neatly wrapped in brown paper. He laid it down gently and scooped out a hole in the filth. With tears in his eyes, he placed the bundle in the hole and covered it.

"Dr. Lai," I asked, "what has he done?"

"I don't know, but I will find out."

He went to the young man and after a brief conversation returned and suggested that we go on our way.

I was insistent, "Dr. Lai, what did he say?"

Dr. Lai replied, "He was burying his son because he did not have money for a funeral."

This incident which I witnessed as a young navy doctor in Tsingtao (since renamed Qingdao), China, left me changed forever and was a determining factor on my journey to India.

---

*Dr. Lai was the competent Chinese official with whom I worked in my duties as battalion sanitation officer with the marines in 1946–47.

Where Is God Not?

I had arrived in China some seven months earlier, having just finished three months indoctrination at the U.S. Naval Hospital at Parris Island, South Carolina. This had followed my graduation from Cornell Medical College in June 1945, and a nine-month surgical internship at Bellevue Hospital in New York City. The navy had then called me to active duty and sent me to Parris Island. From there I was ordered to Hawaii for further assignment. Before I had time to enjoy this island paradise, the navy flew me along with other doctors to China to relieve those whose terms were about to expire.

After nearly two days on the slow transport plane, we landed at Tientsin (now called Tianjin). In that August of 1946 China was in the throes of the civil war between the Communists under Mao Tse-tung (Mao Zedong) and the Nationalists led by Chiang Kai-shek. The city was under siege by the former.

As we were being driven into the city in the back of an armed truck, one of my traveling companions flicked his cigarette butt into the street. Immediately several scrawny coolies jumped for it. As we later learned, the tobacco from seven such butts was enough to make a new cigarette that could be sold for a few pennies. This was my introduction to third-world poverty.

Having requested posting to Peking (Beijing), the navy sent me in the opposite direction, to the marine dispensary in Tsingtao.

Before World War II, Tsingtao had been China's second largest seaport as well as a major resort city. Located on Kaiochow Bay on the Yellow Sea, 350 miles north of Shanghai, it boasted a large natural harbor and miles and miles of wide clean sandy beaches. Years of Japanese occupation followed by bloody civil war had turned the city into a sanctuary for tens of thousands of forgotten refugees from the surrounding countryside.

They lived where they could, some in rude shacks, others in caves carved out of the hills. Having few, if any, possessions and little work, they stole from our naval supply depots. Many were shot, but others kept on trying, for they were desperate and had nothing to lose but their lives.

Duties for the naval doctors were light and the hours short—from 7:00 A.M. to 1:00 P.M. Afternoons we played volleyball or swam and sunbathed on the beaches. With Barbara back in New York City, I soon tired of this, and got permission to work in the local government hospital where help was badly needed. On the wards I saw patients with exotic diseases such as kala-azar and schistosomiasis, diseases that were but footnotes in Western textbooks. A New Zealand surgeon working under the auspices of the United Nations Relief and Rehabilitation Agency (UNRRA) befriended me and invited me to help him in the operating room. This was a fantastic experience, for patient after patient was admitted in all stages of disease or suffering from massive injuries.

He was plagued by severe shortages, particularly of surgical gloves. To sterilize the few pairs available, we soaked them in a solution of bichloride of mercury between operations. While they were still wet, we put them on for the next operation and squeezed out the excess fluid, letting it run down our arms. At the end of the day our hands were wrinkled and resembled those of cadavers. It made me aware that there were urgent needs in places far from home.

In addition to other duties, I was in charge of inspecting restaurants to find out if they were safe for American servicemen. We worked with the local health authorities and learned that they had limited an outbreak of cholera to thirteen cases and had immunized nearly two-thirds of the city of 800,000. It was an impressive performance considering the conditions. In turn, we helped them control mosquitoes by aerial spraying and by immunizing the people in areas where typhus had been detected. It was through these activities that I had met Dr. Lai, a very pleasant and well-educated gentleman.

In the summer of 1947 we received a letter from Dr. Hyla Watters, a Methodist missionary in Wuhu in Anhwei province. She had been a favorite student of my father at Cornell and a visitor to our home on her furloughs. She wrote that she had met Dr. Lai and he had predicted that I would become a missionary.

CHAPTER 2

Welcome to India

THE HAWK SWOOPED DOWN FROM BEHIND, STEALING the cracker from Barbara's hand as we sat drinking tea on the deck of the *Steel Age*. We were anchored in Bombay harbor, the shore a tantalizing hundred yards away. We had finally reached India.

It was late December 1953. The SS *Steel Age*, a small freighter of the Isthmian line, had been our home for five weeks on our trip from New York. Our journey had been uneventful, with stops at Beirut, Lebanon, and Alexandria, Egypt, in the Mediterranean. From there we went through the Suez Canal to Djbouti, French Somaliland, Karachi, Pakistan, and finally Bombay. By now we were tired of our cramped stateroom. With limited space for our active three-year-old son, Bobby, and his six-year-old sister, Carol, to play, it had been harder for them than for us.

The next morning we lifted anchor and moved to the dock. Pacing up and down on the shore was an elderly Indian gentleman with four dozen roses in his arms. He signaled that he was there to meet us. Because of a dispute between the seamen and the dock workers, our debarkation was delayed some three hours during which the roses drooped progressively and finally totally lost heart in the 95 degrees heat. When we left our ship for the last time, he gave us the roses and introduced himself. He was Dr. Balu, the father of Dr. Balu Sankaran,* a resident in orthopedic surgery whom I had met at Presbyterian Hospital. Dr. Balu had come by train from Madras to meet his son's friend. Since the trip took some fifteen hours, we appreciated this friendly welcome and never forgot it.

Before he left us, Dr. Balu took me aside and gave me a safety pin. He showed me how to close my trouser pocket from the inside to thwart pickpockets. His advice was followed for many years whenever we traveled.

Unfortunately, the dispute on the docks had delayed the unloading, and we were unable to clear our baggage that day as planned.

Rev. Harry Shaw, the Presbyterian representative in Bombay, had arranged for us to stay at the Airlines Hotel. That night we had our first taste of Indian curry. Although the waiter assured us that it had few spices, our tongues told us otherwise and we drank gallons of water.

At six the next morning there was a knock on our door and a waiter entered, bringing us tea and crackers. We had not asked for room service, and had no wish to eat at that early hour. But we did, and enjoyed our small repast. After washing up, we went to clear our luggage through customs. As we passed the dining room, the waiter asked if we wanted breakfast. We replied that we had already had it in our room. He corrected us—we had been served *chota hazri* meaning "little breakfast" and often called "bed tea." This was our introduction to this pleasant custom, one that we later modified and adopted.

As we stepped off the curb to cross the street, I heard a shout—"Watch out or you will be killed!"

A taxi bore down on us at breakneck speed from our right. We had forgotten that traffic in India keeps to the left.

After clearing customs we went sightseeing, visiting the famous gardens on Malabar Hill. The beautiful and exotic tropical flowers enchanted us, while the bushes and shrubs shaped in the forms of animals amused the children.

---

*Dr. Balu Sankaran later became the director general of the Indian Health Services.

Where Is God Not?

Two days later we boarded the train for the long journey north, a trip that lasted two nights and a day. We were to go to the town of Kalka where we would be met and taken to Jubar.

No one had warned us that we were expected to provide our own bedding on the train. Nor did we realize how cold northern India would be at the end of December. The compartment was unheated and drafty, with soot from the steam locomotive seeping in around the windows. The wooden seats on which we slept were hard and cold. Fortunately, we had two blankets with us and the children wore their snowsuits. We shivered all night, both nights.

Mr. Budh Ram, the manager of the sanatorium, an elderly and strict orthodox Hindu gentleman, met us in Kalka. What his thoughts were, we shall never know, for he was much too polite to let them show. I have little doubt that he was disappointed by my youthful appearance.

Kalka lay at an elevation of twenty-five hundred feet at the foot of the Himalayan mountains. It was a town of about five thousand, and the railhead where standard gauge trains ended. From there travelers could proceed north either by road or on a narrow gauge railway to Simla, the former summer capital of India, passing through 101 tunnels and climbing an additional five thousand feet on its slow sixty-five-mile trip. Due to the many curves and switchbacks, the trip took an exhausting eight hours and most travelers elected to go by road, either hiring a taxi or on a bus.

Mr. Budh Ram had arranged a taxi to take us twenty-two miles to Jubar. As we passed through Kalka we came face to face with the sacred nature of cows when we saw one that had lost its right front leg. She hobbled around the streets, surviving on the largess of the shopkeepers. She knew which of them would feed her and visited them on a regular basis. For many years she was a constant sight on our frequent trips through the town.

The first few miles up the Simla road were so desolate as to make us want to turn back. We had to remind ourselves that it was winter and would look better in summer. The road climbed steadily, often at grades of 9 percent or more. We counted the twenty-eight twists and turns it made every mile, living up to its reputation for making even the hardiest of travelers carsick.

After sixteen miles we turned left off the main road to Simla and three miles later came to the small village of Garkhal. There the houses perched precariously on the steep hillside and the paved road ended. From Garkhal the road degenerated into a narrow dirt byway for the last three miles to Jubar.

CHAPTER 3

Christmas

AS OUR TAXI ROUNDED THE FINAL BEND, WE SAW THE SIGN—
Lady Irwin Sanatorium. At last we had reached our destination.

Before we had left home, we had searched every available
map of India for Jubar. When we asked Mr. Budh Ram where
Jubar was, he answered that we had just passed it. "But," we
replied, "there were only three houses back there."

"That's Jubar," he said.

The Lady Irwin Tuberculosis Sanatorium lay in the middle of
a beautiful pine forest—a "jungle," to use the Indian term. It
occupied the only level ground along a narrow mountain ridge,
five thousand feet above sea level. The house that was to be our
new home was a quarter-mile away, up a steep and narrow foot
path two hundred feet higher, overlooking the hospital.
Everything, including water, had to be carried there by hand or
on the backs of coolies. It was Christmas Eve when we arrived.
Our luggage had been delayed in transit, not to catch up with us
for another ten days.

Our new home was a massive two-story building, built—as
were all the hospital buildings—of granite quarried on the sanatorium grounds. The rooms were spacious with high ceilings;
most had fireplaces seemingly designed to emit as little heat as
possible. Floors were of cement, without rugs. The furniture was
rickety and threatened to collapse. The roof was made of sheets

of corrugated iron. When hail rattled on the roof, conversation was impossible.

That first night was an ordeal. Our new home was on the top of the ridge, exposed to bitter winter winds that swept over it from all sides, chilling us to the core. The window sashes were loose, admitting large volumes of unwanted frigid air. At night the stairs creaked, frightening all of us, for we knew nothing of the people and worried about thieves.

We borrowed sheets and blankets from the hospital, but they were inadequate for the penetrating cold. Bobby and Carol wore slippers, undershirts, pajamas, and bathrobes when they went to bed. We wore nearly as much. Daytime seemed warmer, providing we remained in the sun. However, whenever a cloud perched on our mountaintop, we shivered.

Our children were only three and six years old when we arrived in India.

Where Is God Not?

It was black outside at five the next morning when we were awakened by singing. The nurses were celebrating Christmas, singing carols on their way to the wards to proclaim the glory of Christ's birth. They invited us to join in the traditional noontime Christmas feast for the entire hospital.

They offered to cook "English" food for us, but we declined, preferring to eat what the others did. The nurses assured us that they had limited the spices for our sake. Although we picked numerous peppercorns out of the rice and curry, our tongues smarted and we could eat little.

Everyone received us warmly, and the children were particularly welcome. We felt wanted.

That first day brought a portent of what much of our medical work would be like.

A woman of uncertain age was brought to the hospital on a *dandy*, a litter designed to allow its four bearers to walk in single file through the jungle. She claimed to be about thirty-five years old, but looked at least twenty more. We examined her and found that she had a hopelessly advanced cervical cancer. The family did not seem surprised or unduly upset when we told them that she was incurable and nothing could be done for her. They said that was her *kismet* or fate, long predetermined, and nobody could change it. After giving her analgesics, we sent her home to die, depressed by her hopelessness.

That night we were nearly ready to go home. But we didn't. We had made a commitment to stay for three years and we intended to honor it. It was also obvious that there was a tremendous lack of medical care in the area.

We felt needed.

CHAPTER 4

Jubar

THE HOSPITAL PRESENTED A CHALLENGE.

It was in a desperate condition, with only seventeen patients housed in two long wards. The long sides were open to the elements and the harsh winter winds blew through them, encouraging patients to stay in bed. Over the years, gifts from friends in America made it possible to enclose the wards, making difficult conditions more bearable.

There were three other wards, all empty.

Scattered around the hillside were twenty small buildings, open to the elements on two or three sides. Each had an attached bathroom and a small room for cooking. These had been built for patients willing and able to pay for a measure of privacy. All were empty.

Monkeys roamed freely, the brown rhesus occasionally darting into the wards to steal food from the patients. They provided a diversion, for few of the patients could read, and none had a radio. Other much larger monkeys with long tails—black-faced grey langurs—were much shyer, and generally kept to the trees. They were more destructive, however, and broke branches as they leaped great distances from tree to tree. When they landed on the galvanized iron roofs, the noise reverberated through the rooms beneath.

The sanatorium generated its own electricity. It had two generators, one an old British-made one-cylinder machine large enough to supply the entire compound with a 220-volt current. The other, much smaller, was of Italian origin and barely adequate for taking x-rays or for use while performing an operation. It generated a current of 170 volts that was then converted to 220 volts. It, too, was old. Both were diesel-operated. Since the nearest source of fuel was twenty-two miles away in Kalka, they were used sparingly.

Medical facilities included a World War II surplus portable x-ray machine of limited capacity, a modest laboratory, and a small but adequate pharmacy. Intravenous fluids were prepared in a homemade still, improvised from an old kerosene can. To our surprise, it functioned flawlessly. The operating room had an overhead light that could not be adjusted. Instead, when necessary, the antiquated operating table had to be moved, sometimes during an operation. To raise one end or tilt the table, an assistant lifted one end or side while another put wooden blocks under its legs. The single spotlight was an automobile headlight mounted on a homemade stand connected to a car battery.

The wards were open to the elements on two sides.

Patients provided their own bedding and eating utensils. Canvas bags filled with pine needles served as mattresses.

The hospital chapel was small, accommodating about fifty. Worshipers sat on mats on the floor, men on the right, women to the left. To our embarrassment, rickety metal chairs were provided for us in the back. Once when Bobby was sitting on my lap, my chair collapsed in the middle of a Sunday service, landing Bobby and me on the floor to the amusement of all. Great sprays of red and white bougainvillea and climbing roses covered the windows behind the altar.

The staff outnumbered patients two to one. Since our expenses were double our income, we were heading for financial disaster. We had only enough money to pay salaries for the next two months.

I soon found out that I was accountable for finances and administration as well as medical care, and learned what so many of our missionary forebears had before us: we would have to do everything—bookkeeping, answering all the correspondence, supervising repairs and maintenance, designing buildings, worrying about legal matters, and so on. Barbara became my unpaid secretary, and we both struggled with the accounts in a new and strange currency, using pice, annas and rupees. There were four pice in one anna, and sixteen annas in a rupee, making addition and subtraction difficult, and multiplication and division almost impossible. Fortunately in 1957 the Indian government wisely decided to adopt the decimal system.

The change to an easier currency was rumored to have led to discontent among the many beggars in Delhi. Since their benefactors normally gave them the smallest coin, their income went down, for there were now one hundred coins to a rupee instead of sixty-four. Beggars refused to take only one of the new pice, in effect going on strike.*

After we had been in Jubar three weeks, Dr. Frederick Scovel and his wife, Myra, fellow Presbyterian missionaries, invited us to visit them at Ludhiana. We accepted quickly, glad to escape our problems for a few days.

---

*A Hindu friend told us that the orthodox believed that by giving to beggars they acquired merit.

Where Is God Not?

Although Ludhiana was only a hundred miles away, we never considered driving, for the sanatorium had only one vehicle, a Land Rover of ancient vintage. Were we to take it, there would be no transportation available for emergencies. The nearest bus stop was three miles away in Garkhal.

We went to Garkhal where we transferred to a crowded bus for the hair-raising trip down to Kalka. The curves still numbered a nauseating twenty-eight per mile. When passengers became sick, and some did on every trip, they merely leaned out of the nearest window and let loose their stomach contents. We learned to sit as close to the front as possible.

In Kalka we took the only train that went straight through to Ludhiana, one that left at eight in the evening and arrived at three in the morning. To our amazement, many of the college staff had risen and walked the mile and a half to the station to welcome us.

Our three-day stay at Ludhiana was devoted to business on my part and shopping by Barbara. As had been predicted, Dr. Snow, the principal of the Medical College, appreciated the problems we faced in starting major thoracic surgery in Jubar. Without a great deal more equipment and additional trained staff it was impossible.

So it was decided that we would do major lung surgery in Ludhiana and move there the following winter. I was to start a chest clinic and help teach general surgery. This sounded like progress, and we rejoiced that things were moving forward. But we were also to continue to run the sanatorium, something we did until it closed twenty years later.

Clearly, without major changes the sanatorium would have to close, for within a week of our arrival there were only thirteen of the original patients still in the hospital. I had discharged two who did not have tuberculosis, and two others had left on their own.

We considered our options and decided that the only way to attract patients was to offer the best care possible. This would include a good diet, first-rate medical treatment, and advanced surgical procedures.

The typical patient arrived at Jubar grossly underweight and malnourished. Therefore it was necessary to begin with a nutritious diet. The hospital food was poor and the patients constantly complained about it. When I discussed the matter with Mr. Budh Ram, he rightly pointed out that we did not have any money to improve the menu. So we took a loan from the medical college at Ludhiana and told Mr. Budh Ram to go ahead anyway and serve better meals.

Soon our patients were gaining weight satisfactorily and improving rapidly. Tragically, when we met them months or years later, although free of disease, they were much thinner and had lost weight—at home they simply could not afford the same diet.

In the 1950s, surgery for tuberculosis was still in its infancy in India. Almost without exception, surgery was limited to thoracoplasty or minor operations. Thoracoplasty involved the removal of several of a patient's ribs, generally in two or three operations, each being done at intervals of ten days to two weeks. Naturally, patients did not like it. While frequently curative, it often produced deformities of the chest. Without good physiotherapy these could be quite severe. As no physiotherapist was available, we trained one of our nurses in this field.

On the other hand, although not always suitable, surgical resection—removal of all or part of a lung—was a newer and better operation. Only one operation was necessary, and, in addition, it offered a higher cure rate. Unfortunately it was technically more difficult and required additional equipment and staff. If we could establish ourselves in this field, then other doctors would refer patients to us. Or so we hoped. Resections had been attempted only once or twice before in northern India.

CHAPTER 5

Help Comes

TUBERCULOSIS KILLS.

Among the poor and malnourished, it exacted a frightful toll, striking the families that could least afford it. Mimicking other diseases, it was frequently misdiagnosed.

Although easily curable when diagnosed early or when the patient's germs are sensitive to antibiotics, most patients who came to Jubar had already been treated and relapsed at least once. The majority went home well, but tragically others died after long and difficult struggles.

The treatment was lengthy, and patients had to take medicines for many months or even years. Occasionally surgery was necessary. In the 1950s the most infectious patients were isolated when possible. Since this was expensive, few could afford it. Sanatoria throughout the world were forced to rely on government and social agencies for financial help.

Competition among the other sanatoria in the mountains for the limited funds available was keen. Although we had done several operations successfully at Ludhiana, we had no reliable base of support. Amazingly, this came about because of Mrs. Roma Chauhan's misfortune.

Raj Kumari Amrit Kaur, one of Mahatma Gandhi's disciples, was the Union Minister of Health. She was a committed

Christian and a close friend of Dr. Snow. When her niece, Mrs. Chauhan, developed tuberculosis she turned to Dr. Snow for advice. The latter said that a new and well-qualified doctor had just arrived from America and was in charge of the Lady Irwin Sanatorium. This suited Mrs. Chauhan as she wanted to be treated in a Christian hospital if possible.

When she and her husband arrived at Jubar, she chose a private cottage rather than the general ward. After seeing her settled comfortably, Mr. Chauhan and I went to the office to discuss her treatment. Fortunately her prognosis seemed favorable, although as I explained to him, she might need an operation later.

Mr. Chauhan received the news without comment. When I suggested that we discuss this with his wife, he objected.

"Dr. Eggleston, you are new to India and do not yet know our customs. Let me give you some advice. You should always tell patients that they will get well. You must never give them bad news. Please don't tell my wife how long she will need treatment or that she might need an operation."

This was totally foreign to my experience, for we had always tried to be honest with our patients, softening bad news with compassion. I thought of the verse, "You will know the truth and the truth will make you free" (John 8:32).

I pointed out to Mr. Chauhan that to get his wife's cooperation we needed her confidence and could have it only if she believed us. After considerable discussion, he agreed to let us outline our treatment plan for her. We walked back to her cottage and discussed it with her. She seemed relieved to be told the truth and accepted it quietly. Mrs. Chauhan ultimately did need surgery.

Learning that the supply of electricity to our operating room in Ludhiana was erratic, Mr. Chauhan, a ranking government official, arranged to be transferred to Ludhiana. There he served as Additional District Magistrate, a position of considerable authority. When the day came for his wife's operation, he issued orders that there were to be no interruptions in the electrical supply to the hospital.

Where Is God Not?

Her operation taught me an important medical lesson, one not in American textbooks. The surgery had gone well and we had no reason to expect any complications. However on the fifth day after surgery she developed a fever. This persisted and gradually rose over the next few days. She had no signs of infection, or any other complication. Finally, the laboratory reported that they had seen malarial parasites in her blood. Treatment was prompt and effective. This was my introduction to the problem of postoperative malaria.

Because of the success of her treatment, Mrs. Chauhan convinced Raj Kumari to have the central (federal) government help our sanatorium. They agreed to support sixty patients, all refugees from Pakistan, and all poor and most malnourished. Since our sanatorium was the only one providing modern surgery, other government hospitals soon began referring patients to us. This allowed us to develop the first training program in chest surgery in North India.

The fact that we told patients the truth about their condition soon became known and patients who were discharged from neighboring sanatoria came to see us, bringing their x-rays with them, asking for a second opinion. This was a major embarrassment, but we could hardly turn them away. Occasionally, we recommended further medical treatment or even surgery.

Because tuberculosis was so prevalent, most patients were treated by general practitioners in villages far from the few specialists in the government-run tuberculosis clinics. Treatment was changing rapidly, with new drugs becoming available and surgical operations safer and more effective. As it was difficult for doctors to keep up-to-date, we hoped to develop programs to help them. The first opportunity came as the result of a letter from Jee Ram.

Jee Ram came to Jubar from a tiny village near New Delhi, 130 miles away. He was a tall, thin, hardworking farmer, emaciated by far-advanced tuberculosis. We had treated him successfully with drugs followed by an operation, for which he was deeply grateful. Shortly after he returned home, a letter arrived, signed "Jee Ram of Jubar." Could his doctor, Suran Das, come and learn more about the treatment of tuberculosis?

Enthusiastically, we wrote back telling Suran Das to meet me in Ludhiana.

At the appointed time, a young man came to our house and introduced himself as Dr. Suran Das. He seemed younger than expected, so I asked him how old he was. He replied that he was nineteen.

Curiosity got the better of me.

"How could you graduate from medical college, since the youngest legal age possible is twenty-one?"

After an embarrassing silence, he replied, "Well, I didn't go to your type of medical college, I went to an *ayurvedic* (an indigenous system of medicine) medical college."

"But, even then, you seem very young to have completed the course."

After an even longer and more awkward pause, he said, "Well, I did not actually graduate."

I persisted, "How far in the course did you get?"

"I completed most of the first year of study and then dropped out because I could not afford to continue."

Hiding my astonishment with difficulty, I told him that the only way the Christian Medical College could help him was if he became a qualified doctor. He had anticipated this, and took the rejection graciously.

Upon further questioning I learned that he was the only "doctor" for thirty-five miles around his village. Patients such as Jee Ram considered him their doctor, and why not? There was no one else available. Possibly he was better than nobody. But we wondered.

Many patients came to Jubar on their own. Some could pay our full charges, others could afford only their food and medicines. A few were destitute and were given free treatment. No one was ever turned away.

Mirchu Ram was typical. He worked as a coolie on a construction site far to the west. When he first arrived at Jubar he was skin and bones, coughing blood, his disease far advanced. He was desperately poor, with a wife and two children dependent upon him. We admitted him and charged him only the cost of his food. Even then, he stayed but two months, barely long enough to improve slightly, gain a few pounds and recover some strength. Then he left, to go back to his physically demanding work.

He returned the next three summers, repeating the same performance, his condition gradually deteriorating and his germs becoming resistant to all medicines. The hospital staff was concerned, for one could only imagine what would happen to his family when he died.

We offered to treat him for nothing if he would stay long enough to be cured—if that were still possible. He thanked us, but pointed out that each winter he saved enough money for his family to survive for the two months he spent with us, after which he had to leave to earn enough for the following year. The obvious answer was to support him and his family. But the hospital had barely enough money to stay open, let alone consider such a possibility. In addition, if we did it for one patient, another hundred would soon be on our doorstep.

We wept for the poor of India and felt helpless.

The few patients who could afford treatment (the all-inclusive charges were $1.18 per day), often refused to stay long enough to get completely well. Sometimes those who could afford to stay went home when they began to feel better, claiming that we wanted to keep them unnecessarily for the sake of income.

Others who could leave were advised to continue their treatment at home. Whenever possible, they were referred to clinics near their homes where facilities were available. Too often they returned six months or a year later in worse condition, having stopped their medicines because of the inconvenience or the cost. Others simply refused to accept the need for long-term treatment. It was discouraging work, for there were no social service agencies available for follow-up or to help patients.

Others came to us only because they could no longer cope at home and finally agreed to be hospitalized. A few were sent by relatives concerned lest other members of their families became infected. Tragically, sometimes they found out that it was too late—they too were infected.

A few patients arrived with very far advanced or incurable disease, were treated, improved a bit, and then went home expecting to die. Months later, they returned to Jubar in an even worse state and died on our wards. Since the Hindu community felt it a disgrace to die in a hospital, we were at a loss to understand why they insisted on returning. When we asked them, they told us that it was because of the compassionate and loving Christian care given by our nursing staff. They wanted to be surrounded by people who cared for them and were not afraid to be with them as they died.

CHAPTER 6

The Hand of God

IT WAS EARLY EASTER MORNING 1955 WHEN THE TELEPHONE rang.

I hurried down to the hospital to find Dr. Edward Ingram on the other end of the line. "Please can you help?"

"What is the problem?"

"Jim Ashwin has polio and is getting worse rapidly."

We were in Jubar celebrating Christ's resurrection with the staff and patients. Dr. Ingram, a surgeon at the medical college at Ludhiana, was calling from Simla, eighty-odd miles beyond Jubar in the Himalayas. A few days earlier he and Jim Ashwin, a colleague from Ludhiana, had gone there for a brief vacation. The night before the call, Ashwin had developed symptoms of polio and his condition was deteriorating.

Fortunately, we had borrowed a colleague's van to go to Jubar, because our temperamental secondhand Dodge was being repaired for the umpteenth time. We sent the van with a driver and a nurse to bring Ashwin to Jubar.

When they returned some eight hours later, it was obvious that the situation was critical. Ashwin's condition was worsening and his level of paralysis rising. Clearly he would soon need a respirator.

There were no respirators in the Simla Hills. Delhi was far away and we did not know which if any hospitals had a one. Dr.

Snow had mentioned that Lord Nuffield was said to have donated an "iron lung" to all mission hospitals in India. I had seen one at Ludhiana and one at the mission hospital in Ambala, some fifty-five miles to the south. As far as we knew, neither had ever been used. Ambala was contacted, but their doctors said they had never used it and did not know if it was functional.

I debated calling Ludhiana, for there was an inviolate rule—Sunday was a day of rest and virtually every activity was forbidden. Even the net on the tennis court was taken down. There was no telephone in the hospital, only one in the principal's office in the college. It was not to be answered on the Sabbath. It seemed fruitless to call.

But there was no other place where we could take Ashwin. I was desperate, and after prayer, in desperation I did call the local telephone operator and ask her to call Ludhiana.

To my great surprise, Dr. Snow answered. "What is it?"

"This is Forrest. I'm in Jubar and Jim Ashwin has polio. He is getting worse and needs a respirator."

"Bring him here to Ludhiana. We haven't used our iron lung in many years, but will try to get it ready."

Wondering what to expect at Ludhiana, in desperation we put Ashwin on a stretcher in the back of the van, and Ingram and I set off. We arrived at two the next morning. Dr. Ronald Garst, the friend who had loaned us the van, had worked hard and gotten the iron lung in working condition.

Within a matter of hours Ashwin was to need it. He remained on it for many weeks.

Several weeks later I asked Dr. Snow how she had come to answer the telephone that time, for she was adamant about not working Sunday.

She answered, "As you know, I had expressly forbidden the use of the phone on Sunday. But that day when I heard it ringing as I passed by my office door, I felt an overwhelming compulsion and I simply had to answer it. So despite my belief that I should not, I did."

God had answered my prayer.

CHAPTER 7

Holy Cow

THE PLACE TO WHICH GOD CALLED US WAS AWE-INSPIRING—
the mighty Himalayas, the rooftop of the world.

From the top of the hill behind our house we could see the
plains of North India spread out before us to the south and the
west. On clear nights, the lights of Chandigarh, the new capital
of Punjab State, twinkled below, and one could dimly imagine
the glow of Ludhiana far to the west. To the north and east, eter-
nally snowcapped peaks soared, many rising to twenty thousand
feet or more. In the evenings they blazed red in the sunsets.
When low clouds swept over the valleys below, they engulfed the
sanatorium beneath our house, leaving only the tips of the
mountains visible far in the distance.

In the surrounding forest, layer upon layer of pine needles
blanketed the ground. During the dry season they caught fire
and burned around the hospital. With great foresight those who
came before us had replaced most of the pine trees near the
buildings with other trees, sparing us this danger.

A few panthers still roamed the surrounding hillsides as well
as animals that the local people called hyenas. Shortly after our
arrival our pharmacist's large German shepherd was killed by
one of them.

Gohs, shy, dragon-like animals, probably members of the
family of monitor lizards, lived underground in rocky areas. Very

quick when cornered, they would climb trees or turn on their tormentors, hissing and sticking out long forked tongues. They grew to well over four feet in length and ate chickens and other small animals.

Birds were a constant source of delight. Brown Himalayan tree-pies, with foot-long tails and liquid calls, vied for our attention as did red-billed blue magpies with even longer tails. Occasionally blue-crested paradise flycatchers flitted through the trees, their long white tails trailing behind them. During the spring mating season cuckoos called to each other.

Water was scarce and the hospital relied on rain water as well as its own spring. This lay on an adjacent mountain more than a mile away and five hundred feet higher than the hospital. A single one-inch pipe fed our storage tanks by gravity. Rain was collected from the roofs in large old and rusty tanks scattered around the compound. The supply was limited and when the monsoons failed, as they frequently did, the flow from the spring decreased to a trickle and the rain barrels no longer filled. Water, or rather the lack of it, was a constant concern. At times our family lived on a daily ration of five gallons per person.

To conserve water we used it sparingly and, when possible, more than once. When we scrubbed our hands before an operation, we put a plug in the sink, to save the water. This was then used to give a preliminary rinse to the soiled linen. What was left then served to water our small garden.

Gauze bandages and dressings were washed, resterilized, and used over and over until reduced to shreds. Pills were dispensed in old envelopes, and liquids in bottles that were recycled. Patients frequently brought their own bottles with them when they needed refills.

Although primarily a tuberculosis sanatorium, we hoped that Jubar would also serve as a general hospital for the surrounding community. There was a great need for this, for the nearest medical facilities were two government hospitals six and nine miles to the east and a third twenty-five miles to the west. All were understaffed and inadequately equipped.

Gaining public acceptance proved easier than expected. We had been in Jubar less than two months when on a dreary damp

Where Is God Not?

Saturday afternoon, Bhagwant Lal came to the hospital. He sought out Mr. Silas, the pharmacist, and asked for a mustard plaster for his brother, Kastori Lal, who was dying. Mr. Silas referred him to me.

"Why don't you bring Kastori Lal to the hospital?"

"There is no point, Kastori Lal is beyond hope. Besides which we live three miles beyond Jagjitnagar. It's too far."

Bhagwant Lal returned home disappointed when we refused his request as we did not want to encourage villagers to use the hospital as a drug store.

Early Sunday morning, Bhagwant Lal reappeared, this time accompanied by others of the family.

One of them spoke. "Kastori Lal is worse. Please reconsider and give us a mustard plaster."

"No. The best thing is for you to bring him here to the hospital. If you won't do that, I can go to his home and examine him."

After a long consultation, they agreed to my seeing him in his home. A fee of 10 rupees ($2.35) was set.

Taking a few medicines along with us, Sister Taj James,* our senior Indian nurse, and I set out in the hospital Land Rover, Barbara and the children accompanying us for the ride. After a bumpy and twisty three miles, the dirt road ended abruptly at the tiny village of Jagjitnagar. We walked another three miles through the forest, enjoying spectacular views of the mountains to the north and the plains to the south. Finally, we reached a cluster of ten or twelve small houses. We were ushered into one, no larger than eight by ten feet. Sitting bolt upright on a *charpoy* (an Indian rope bed) was a fifty-year-old man, gasping for breath. The floor was covered with black spots until one of the men waved his hand and the flies flew away only to settle elsewhere.

It was hard to see anything, for the door and the single barred window were packed with the curious. The entire village wondered what this foreign doctor could or would do.

I turned to Kastori Lal. "Please take off your shirt."

With great reluctance, he obliged.

---

*The term "sister" was used for senior nurses, a custom no doubt acquired from the British.

Diagnosis was obvious; Kastori Lal had simple heart failure, a condition that we could treat easily.

Sister Taj spoke up. "Kastori Lal, get dressed and your friends can take you to our Land Rover. We can then bring you to the hospital."

"No" was the emphatic response.

Bhagwant Lal took Sister Taj aside. "We will be disgraced if he dies in the hospital. Dr. Eggleston can give him medicine, but that is all."

The only suitable medicine that we had in our pharmacy was digitalis, an excellent and potent drug, but one that could be dangerous unless given properly. Some one would have to check Kastori Lal's pulse periodically. In addition, the hospital did not have any of the newer forms of the drug, but only a tincture that had to be administered drop-wise. We had none with us; the family would have to get it from the hospital. Since the dose depended on Kastori Lal's pulse rate, I asked, "Who has a watch?" No one had one. Finally, after we had emphasized that without one we could not treat Kastori Lal at home, an old man produced one, but one without a second hand. So Sister Taj again said that Kastori Lal would have to go to the hospital. Finally another man stepped forward, and he had a watch, one with a second hand.

With the entire village watching closely, we taught Bhagwant Lal how to take a pulse. After several practice sessions we were satisfied that he could do it accurately.

Taking Bhagwant Lal with us, we returned to Jubar. We gave him a bottle of tincture of digitalis and a medicine dropper and taught him how to measure the drops into a glass of water. I stressed that digitalis was a very potent drug, and that giving more than needed was more dangerous than giving too little. With a simple chart telling how many drops to give Kastori Lal every morning after taking his pulse, Bhagwant Lal went home.

We prayed that Bhagwant Lal would follow our instructions. If he thought that giving more medicine than ordered would make Kastori Lal recover sooner, he might kill Kastori Lal. We were not certain that we had been completely understood.

Where Is God Not?

One week later Kastori Lal walked into the sanatorium. Our reputation was established and we were accepted.

I wondered what my teachers at Cornell would have thought.

As a result of our new-found fame, a few days later a call came for me to go to the hospital to see a very different type of patient. Standing stolidly in front of the office was a cow with a large swelling in her neck. The owner asked me to drain what he thought was an abscess.

The cow stared unhappily at me. My experience as a veterinarian was limited to the usual laboratory experiments on frogs, dogs, cats, and turtles at Cornell. While the unfortunate cow might have had an abscess, I was not certain if the diagnosis was correct. In addition, I had no idea of what anesthesia to give or how much. I also did not relish the possibility of being kicked or bitten for my efforts.

Recalling the sacred nature of cows, I wanted no part of this challenge, and declined to treat this "patient." Instead, we suggested that they take her across the valley to a government veterinary hospital. When they left, the cow seemed as relieved as I was.

Soon more suitable patients began coming.

A Clubfoot

DURGA DAS'S BABY WAS SIX MONTHS OLD WHEN SHE brought it to the hospital for the first time. The child had been born with a clubfoot. Although treatment should have begun earlier, we were delighted that Durga Das had not waited any longer. Enthusiastically we applied the necessary plaster cast and emphasized the need to bring the child back at regular intervals.

This Durga Das did faithfully for several months, the child's foot gradually improving.

Then she failed to return on schedule. We waited a few days but were concerned. The child's foot was continuing to grow, the cast could not and the baby might be permanently crippled.

Fortunately, Sister Taj knew the village where Durga Das lived and went and sought her out.

"Why did you not return?"

Durga Das's reply was quick in coming. "I would have, but my landlord told me that I must not. He said that God had given my child a clubfoot and I had no right to interfere."

Sister Taj talked persuasively, and overcame Durga Das's concern about her God. The child returned for further treatment.

After several more visits, Durga Das again failed to bring her child back. Again Sister Taj went to the village. Durga Das had removed the cast herself. When Sister Taj asked her why she did not come back to the hospital, the latter said that her landlord had convinced her that she need not.

Where Is God Not?

"Why?"

"The child is only a girl. Why bother?"

We never saw the child again.

I thought of our daughter and our love and concern for her and compared it with Durga Das's indifference. Was this the result of her religion or the culture in which she lived? It was both. Barbara and I found it difficult to understand. Tragically, such incidents were repeated time and again. Cultural and religious habits constantly interfered with our attempts to practice medicine as we knew it. It was frustrating, but did make us feel more needed than ever. However, we never learned to accept these habits.

Another patient was the Raja of Kutar. Kutar had been one of the hundreds of princely states that was absorbed into India in 1947. It had been a very small one, probably less than twenty-five square miles in size. One of the poorest states, it was made up of marginal farms, surrounded by mountains with a gap in the west where the Sutlej river flowed down to the plains. Its palace hardly merited the title, being merely a large building with ten or fifteen rooms at best.

When the Raja suddenly started vomiting large quantities of blood, he sent for every doctor in the area to attend him. When my turn came, the Raja sent a horse to fetch me. The idea of riding the horse down the steep mountainside did not appeal to me, so again I drove to Jagjitnagar and walked two miles down to the floor of the valley.

I was ushered into the presence of the Raja. Six months earlier, his only son, aged nineteen, had died suddenly. Always a heavy drinker the Raja had been drinking continuously ever since.

My examination showed that he had cirrhosis of the liver and was bleeding severely from his esophagus. He needed blood and possibly an operation. Since there were no facilities for any of this within a hundred miles, I offered to arrange for an ambulance to take him to Ludhiana. However, he declined and elected to follow the advice of Dr. Kahn, a doctor friend from Subathu, a nearby village. The latter had recommended a cough syrup.

Two days later the Raja was dead.

Considering the conditions at the time, Dr. Kahn's treatment was probably as effective as ours would have been.

In June we decided to open a weekly clinic at Jagjitnagar and asked the local *panchayat* (a local government consisting of five persons, generally men) for help. They offered us the use of two small rooms in the basement of an unused, cold, dank building.

We prepared boxes of drugs and bandages, organized a small portable laboratory, and set forth.

On our way we passed a tiny stream. Beside it sat a woman holding an infant on her lap so that water trickled backward over its forehead. We asked her what she was doing, and why. She explained that every summer she gave her child this treatment for two hours weekly. This she said would protect it from illness the following winter.

Our first clinic was a great success. In accordance with local custom, the panchayat wreathed us with garlands. We then drank quantities of strong tea and listened to speeches and offers of help. We treated well over 180 patients, many of whom no doubt had come out of curiosity.

After five weeks of this stimulating and useful work, a drenching monsoon rain washed the road to oblivion, and we were forced to close the clinic. It no longer mattered, for people now realized that we were there to serve them and they came to the hospital in ever increasing numbers. Not only did patients come from nearby, they came from far distances, often walking tens of miles. Others arrived in dandys, a few were carried in baskets or on the backs of their relatives.

Occasionally we were called to see patients in nearby hospitals. We did this only with the permission and knowledge of the other doctors involved.

Piara Das came to Jubar asking us to see his brother, Ramji Das. The latter had been admitted to the local civil (government) hospital in Kasauli a week earlier because of acute pain in his abdomen. He had been gradually improving until that morning when he collapsed.

We drove to Kasauli, a town of some five thousand, three miles beyond Garkhal and about a thousand feet higher than Jubar. The road ran through a pine forest, overlooking the valley two thousand feet below. In good weather we always enjoyed the drive, although it took half an hour to go the six miles because of the twists and turns in the road. During the monsoon we dreaded the trip, for our Land Rover was old and its canvas cover leaked copiously. Furthermore, the first three miles to Garkhal were on a dirt road made slippery by pine needles. The government hired three coolies to maintain the road, but they were rarely to be found.

A chair blocked the road in Garkhal outside the Delhi Cloth House. The proprietor was a friend of ours and had the only telephone in the village. He used this simple method to let us know that there was a message from the hospital for us. This time it was to pick up a package. On other occasions it might be to see a patient and spare him or her the three-mile walk to Jubar.

While our driver went for the package, I wandered down the narrow lane, hoping to buy some *burphee*, a tasty candy made of milk and sugar. To my disappointment, there was none available. The shopkeeper suggested *jalabies*. These candies were made from a batter of flour and yoghurt with a pinch of saffron, deep fried and then dipped in a sugary syrup. They were very good when fresh. As these were not fresh and covered with flies, I decided against them. Nearby was a glass case in which they could have been kept clean. When I pointed this out to him, the shopkeeper said it would not work—if there were no flies on the jalabies, people could not know they were sweet and would not buy them.

I decided to stick to surgery and leave public health to others.

Dr. Sunder Ram, the doctor in charge of the civil hospital, was eagerly awaiting us. As we walked to the ward to examine Ramji Das, Dr. Ram told me that he had been admitted with a large and painful lump in his belly, an abscess resulting from an untreated ruptured appendix. Dr. Ram had given the proper treatment and his patient had been slowly improving. The mass had been getting smaller and his fever subsiding. Suddenly that morning he had complained of severe pain in his abdomen, developed a high fever, and collapsed. The lump was no longer present. Clearly, the abscess had ruptured, and he now had generalized peritonitis.

During our discussion, Ramji Das and his relatives had kept quiet. When we asked them if they had noticed anything out of the ordinary, they said no. After persistent questioning, one of them admitted that they had not been satisfied with the slow progress and had called another doctor to see him. Dr. Ram had known nothing of this and wanted to know why it was done without his authorization. He scolded them and said that it was against hospital rules. If they were not satisfied, they should have spoken to him.

"Dr. Sahib,* we knew that you would not approve of our doctor."

"Who was he?"

"It was one from the village."

After further questioning, they admitted that it was not a doctor, but a wrestler whom they had called. Since the family knew that Dr. Ram would never give permission for him to "treat" a patient, the wrestler had sneaked in through a window at two o'clock that morning. He had felt the lump and said that he could remove it. Remove it he did, with vigorous massage, rupturing the abscess, and producing generalized peritonitis.

Dr. Ram was delighted to transfer Ramji Das to Jubar. That evening we operated on him, and after a prolonged convalescence, he recovered.

In many villages around Jubar the local wrestler, being the strongest man, also served as the bonesetter, often with disastrous results.

While the medical activities of wrestlers gradually diminished, other traditional forms of medicine continued to flourish. Many patients with chronic abdominal pain had circular scars on their abdomens, the result of the application of strong and caustic counterirritants.

Not infrequently, villagers, including some of our staff, searched for certain types of milkweed that grew around the hospital. These they took for fever or abdominal pain. We could never learn if it helped or not, although we later treated many of the same patients for malaria or hookworm infestation.

Local treatments were not necessarily harmless, for patients with cancer often relied on them and later came to us in a hopeless condition.

---

*Sahib is a term actually meaning master, and was much used in colonial India as a form of address to the British. Today it is a commonly used term of respect.

Where Is God Not?

Village women worked hard, particularly during the harvest season when their help was needed in the fields. Since they had to take their young children with them, they sometimes gave them opium to keep them quiet. Occasionally a child got too much and was brought to Jubar unconscious. A few died.

In addition to the general medical work, I wanted to develop surgery. Fortunately, my predecessors had also had this interest, and the nurses and one of the orderlies were reasonably well trained in operating-room procedures.

Anesthesia, however, was a problem, and the medical college too far away to provide help. Although Mr. Silas had completed a course in the subject, he did not feel adequately qualified.

While most operations could be done under local or spinal anesthesia, others needed general anesthesia. Although Barbara was a trained nurse, she had no experience in this field. I pressed her into service, using only simple and relatively safe drugs.

Among her early patients was our son, Bobby. As he was playing one day, we noticed a small lump on his back. Clearly it needed to be removed and I foolishly thought that I could take it out under local anesthesia. Bobby was but three and a half at the time and wriggled so much that finally Barbara had to give him ether. The operation took only a couple of minutes, but it seemed an eternity. Bobby was fine afterwards; we, his parents, were exhausted.

Inadvertently Bobby also brought home to us the value of food. One evening when he misbehaved at the dinner table, we sent him to bed without dessert—to us a mild and well-deserved punishment. Our cook, Yusuf, found out and was very upset. He pointedly asked how we, who had enough to eat, could deprive a member of our own family of food. Since his own children were severely malnourished when they came to Jubar, we understood. Yusuf felt we could physically beat Bobby (we never did), but we must never deprive him of food.

One year while we were away in Ludhiana during Holy Week, unbeknownst to me and without my approval, an overenthusiastic lay preacher was invited to lead a series of meetings. This he did with great fervor. Confined to their beds, the patients could not escape his daily three-hour exhortations. Since only a handful of them were Christian, the rest naturally objected strongly.

They demanded and got an apology, and a guarantee that there would be no repetition.

But eight patients insisted that the doctor who had issued the invitation be fired. Naturally I refused this request. They then went on a hunger strike. Matters continued at an impasse for two days, the eight remaining obdurate, refusing all food.

I had visions of the great (and effective) hunger strikes led by Mahatma Gandhi during the "quit India" movement, strikes that eventually resulted in India's independence. We were worried lest newspapers would play up the story and inflame communal feelings.

Deciding that it must end without physical force, I instructed the cooks that when they distributed the food to the patients, they place it on a table beside the bed of the ringleader. Indian food is aromatic, and its pungent odor made resistance difficult. One meal later the strike was over, and the patients apologized.

Unfortunately, that was not to be our last strike.

CHAPTER 9

Strikes and Unions

KARTAR LAL SWORE AT NURSE MULL. ALL BECAUSE SHE asked him to wait his turn to get his medicine.

In addition to being a patient, he was a policeman, although of questionable character, and thought that he should have special privileges. Dr. Sosomma Matthew, our young but very capable doctor from the state of Kerala in South India, politely asked him to return to his bed. When he refused, she spoke more strongly. Finally he went to his bed, shouting that the doctor had insulted him and I must fire her.

Another patient, Rikki Ram, joined him and the two went to the manager's office. They ordered the latter to send a telegram to the government to let them know that Dr. Matthew had beaten a patient. Since Dr. Matthew was a lady and all of 4 feet 9 inches tall, and Kartar Lal at least a head taller, the manager did not believe them and refused.

Soon a third patient came to my office and announced that six of them were going on a *satyagraha*—or hunger strike. We sent for the ringleader, Rikki Ram, but he refused to come to the office, saying that he was too weak. He said that I must go to the ward to talk to him. Having no intention to oblige him, I had four ward helpers bring him to the office. A healthy-looking Rikki Ram sat before me and ordered me to fire Dr. Matthew. I told him we would not, and that we were discharging him. With newly found strength, he returned to the ward, taking care to stop and roll in a mud puddle. He announced to the other patients that I too had beaten him, and that the mud was proof.

So all six strikers were brought to the office, and with the staff watching, I asked each of them to stop the strike. All refused. We repeated the performance two more times, with the same result.

Since all six were noninfectious and able to continue their treatment on an outpatient basis, we told them that they were now discharged.

Ward aides helped them pack and get ready to leave. By now they had changed their minds, and wanted to apologize. The manager had already notified the agencies supporting them and it was too late. We gave them the necessary medical advice and told them where to go to complete their treatment.

All but Rikki Ram left peacefully. He went to Shaktighat, the neighboring village, and, sitting like a king under a large shade tree, announced that he would fast to death. He soon instigated some of our staff and the leaders of the hospital labor union to demonstrate against me.

The police arrived. The senior officer remarked that he had had tuberculosis several years earlier, and needed a checkup. We took an x-ray and Dr. Matthew examined him. Fortunately, he was in good health. He thanked us and said that he would help us.

After his investigation, he called me and asked, "Doctor, have you or any of your staff beaten any patients?"

I answered, "Do you really think my family and I have left our home and traveled 8000 miles so that I can beat a sick man?"

He said to forget it and went on to warn me, "A few patients and some members of your staff are organizing a parade in protest. You must go to your house and wait until it is over."

I asked, "Where and when are they going to hold this parade?"

"Why do you want to know?"

"Nothing like this has ever happened to me. My wife and I want to take some pictures to show to our future grandchildren."

Where Is God Not?

He asked if we were serious about watching the parade. When I assured him we were, he said that he would inform the strikers. No parade was ever held, almost to my disappointment.

Nothing in my training had prepared me for hospital administration, let alone dealing with labor problems in a foreign land. During all but the first two of the twenty years that we were responsible for the sanatorium there was a labor union.

To compound the problem, members of the local communist party had organized the union and controlled and financed it. While most of the workers had little or no interest in it, they were coerced into joining.

As soon as it was organized, the union demanded an unreasonable increase in pay. We would have liked to give part of it, but the hospital did not have the money. It was losing money and would soon have to borrow more from the medical college just to keep open. Fortunately, only a protest was planned, not a strike.

To emphasize their grievances, the union ordered all workers to wear black arm bands. I was uncertain how to deal with this.

The answer came at lunch through our son. Bobby was then five years old, and everybody's friend. To keep him busy, Daulet Ram, the hospital carpenter and handyman, a kindly man, allowed Bobby to "help" in the maintenance shop. Bobby had seen Daulet Ram wearing a black arm band, and asked him why. Daulet Ram had replied, "To protest unfair working conditions."

Bobby did not understand and at lunch asked, "Daddy, why does Daulet Ram wear a black band on his arm?"

I answered, "I suppose it is to show that he works in the hospital."

Quickly Bobby said, "Then shouldn't I have an arm band too?"

I agreed, and Barbara took an old black sock and sewed it on his shirtsleeve. That afternoon he went back to the workshop, proudly showing it to everybody.

An embarrassed Daulet immediately rolled up his sleeve. The next day all arm bands disappeared.

Unfortunately the union didn't go away so easily.

We were concerned about the needs of our staff, for they were undoubtedly poor and we could never pay them as much as we would have liked. The hospital's major source of income was the central (federal) government, and they reimbursed us at a fixed rate, one that barely covered our costs.

To help the staff, we obtained permission from the local authorities to open a distribution center where the staff could get a limited supply of essential food at prices well below the market rate. We provided them and their families free medical care, no mean benefit, for sickness was a way of life and their family members numerous.

The union, quite naturally, exploited the workers and made unrealistic demands. To aggravate the situation, the leaders complained directly to the State Labor Bureau rather than to us.

On one occasion we were summoned to Garkhal to meet with a government labor conciliator. We were handed a long list of complaints—most of them trivial and easily disposed of. The one that irked me most was a new one—a request for housing allowance for Jee Das, a ward aide. He had been entitled to this for several months but the manager had inadvertently overlooked it. The union had withheld his request deliberately to embarrass us. I told the conciliator that if we been aware of the problem, we would have corrected it. The labor officer agreed that since the union had not told us about it, they did not have the interests of the workers at heart and the union should pay the arrears. We would pay in the future.

The usual request for a salary increase was far beyond our budget. Finally, after a very long and tedious discussion, I announced that we would grant the union its wishes, but the hospital would have to close in two months. The union leader immediately responded, "Then you must give severance pay, for the workers have rights when an institution closes."

The labor officer replied, "You bloody fool, you are not thinking of the workers, for they will all be out of a job, and then what will happen?"

41

Where Is God Not?

Although we won that time, I always regretted not being able to pay them more.

An unwritten but traditional duty of sweepers was to take the bodies of the patients who died to the morgue. This was considered a very degrading job, and no one else would do it.

Early one spring, the sweepers decided that unless they were paid an allowance for this, they would no longer handle the dead. While I was away in Ludhiana they stopped working and went on strike. The manager promptly fired them.

Naturally the union reported this to the government.

I hurried back to Jubar to meet Banarsi Das, a government labor conciliator, who had come from Chandigarh, the state capital, to mediate. He turned out to be a decent young man.

We discussed the situation, and it soon became clear that the manager had not followed the detailed and time-consuming legal steps required for disciplinary action. Banarsi Das warned us that if the union went to court, which they were likely to do, we were certain to lose. Besides reinstating the sweepers, the court would make us give them back pay from the time of the dispute. He reminded us that because of the snail-like pace of the legal process, this might take six to eight years.

Banarsi Das spent the next three hours conferring with the aggrieved sweepers and union representatives. Then we all met together. I never learned what Banarsi Das told the sweepers, but he had persuaded them that it was in the best interests of all for them to return to work, and that I would take them back. They apologized, and the matter was settled.

When we drove back to Ludhiana that evening, Banarsi Das rode with us as far as Chandigarh. On the way we discussed the legal steps we should have followed in disciplining uncooperative or lazy workers. Finally, he turned to me and said, "Doctor, the next time you want to fire someone, give me a call, and I'll help you do it legally."

Fortunately, we never needed his services.

CHAPTER 10

Don't Tell My Wife

"I CAN'T EAT IT."

Daulet Ram was adamant. He would not eat meat.

Daulet was the very capable "mistri" or carpenter at Jubar. Actually, he was far more than that. This lean pleasant worker was also a competent electrician, plumber, mason, and blacksmith. In fact there was little he could or would not do around the hospital. Much of it had been built by him.

Early one spring morning Daulet Ram complained of a sudden severe pain in his left side. He had a kidney stone and needed surgery. Facilities at Jubar being inadequate for such an operation, we took him to Ludhiana.

While evaluating him for surgery, the surgical resident in charge found that his proteins were very low, and suggested that Daulet include some meat in his diet.

Again Daulet said, "I can't eat it. I am a Brahmin."*

The resident replied. "If you are not in good condition, it will not be safe to operate. In fact, we will not operate."

"But then what will happen?"

"Your pain will not get better and you will stay sick. Why not try a little meat?"

"You know I can't."

---

*A Brahmin is a Hindu of the highest caste.

43

Where Is God Not?

"Think of the meat as a medicine. Then maybe you can."

Daulet was torn by indecision. Finally the pain won, and Daulet said he would take meat—providing it was considered medicine.

To his surprise, he found that he liked it.

We removed his stone and he returned to Jubar.

A few months later, I had occasion to go to the workshop while Daulet and his Brahmin companions were preparing their midday meal. On the fire a piece of goat meat was slowly cooking. Daulet became alarmed. "Don't tell my wife. She will never approve, and will make me leave home."

Assuring him that his secret was safe, I left. I had learned the power of the Indian woman in her own home.

While Daulet Ram was willing to compromise his Brahmin traditions concerning his diet, he and the other Brahmins on the staff never ate with the rest of us at the institutional feasts on Christmas and Independence Day. Instead they gathered in the workshop, and cooked their own food over the blacksmith hearth. They always invited Bobby to join them, for he was a boy and often played there. On the other hand, Carol spent more time with the nurses.

Most of our staff were local farmers and simple honest workers. Some worked in the sanatorium for all the forty-five years it was open, depending on it to supplement their meager income, for their fields were small and the soil poor.

The mountains were steep and terraced. Some terraces were too narrow to grow more than one or two rows of corn. In addition, there was a chronic lack of water. When the rains failed, crops shriveled, prices soared, and the people went without.

Families lived together, with several generations under the same roof or in houses nearby. These, in turn, were clustered in groups of four to ten or occasionally more, near their fields. Choice locations were those close to springs of which there were few. Sanitation was nearly nonexistent, the fields providing the necessary facilities. Diseases spread rapidly, particularly during the rainy season.

Refuse was dumped in piles outside buildings, remaining there indefinitely. Flies multiplied. As screening was expensive, it was seldom used.

Houses were made of stone or granite quarried on the site or nearby. Bricks had to be brought in by truck and were expensive and rarely used. Windows were small and few; most had bars for protection. Glass was beyond the means of most, wooden shutters providing protection from the rain and the cold winter winds. Roofs were made of timbers laid over the walls and covered with mud. These served well enough unless the monsoon rains were excessive or the beams had rotted. The houses were probably similar to those in Capernaum where Jesus cured the paralytic (Mark 2:4).

Women cooked on *angithies*, small portable stoves, using locally made charcoal. They started their fires out-of-doors to burn off the first fumes that were not only smoky but often toxic. Unfortunately, during the winter season, an occasional family brought their angithies indoors too soon, and the next morning all would be found dead.

Women wore the *salwar kameez*, not the sari we had expected. This outfit consisted of a longish loose tunic worn over baggy trousers. It was also the dress of most women on the plains in the North. As is ever true about women's dress, styles changed with the years. The length of the kameez or tunic rose and fell, as did the looseness or tightness of the salwar. Along with the salwar kameez went a long scarf called a *chuni* that was sometimes used to cover the head. Barbara soon adopted this sensible dress although she used saris for formal occasions.

Other than moneylenders and shopkeepers, and they were often the same, people were thin and undernourished, for they were poor and life was harsh.

Moneylenders had an invidious reputation for greed and lack of concern. Our staff was constantly in debt to them for loans incurred for marriages or to buy seed or to build their houses.

The interest moneylenders charged was exorbitant, often more than 20 percent a year. Sometimes the original loan had been repaid many times over, yet the remaining debt was larger than ever. In some areas of the country these debts were handed down from one generation to the next, keeping the victims and their children permanently in debt.

Where Is God Not?

Daulet Ram approached me one day, asking for a loan of six hundred rupees to repay Shiv Das, a local shopkeeper and moneylender. The amount was the equivalent of ten months' salary. I suggested that he repay fifty rupees a month, and in a year he would be free of debt. As was the custom, Shiv Das refused, and would only accept full payment in a single installment. To help Daulet Ram, we personally lent him the money. He repaid us within a year.

Other members of the staff learned that we wanted to help them and began pressuring us to lend them money. To solve the problem, we established a loan fund with a reasonable rate of interest.

We also hoped to help our staff advance themselves. Other than the nurses, pharmacist, and manager, none had more than four or five years of schooling or any opportunity to improve his or her lot in life. Most were illiterate.

However, Chand seemed to have potential. Mr. Silas, besides his work as pharmacist, postmaster and x-ray technician, ran our small laboratory. One day he suggested to me that since Chand showed interest and skill in this work, he could be trained as a laboratory technician. This would be a tremendous step up for him. Chand was excited at the idea.

So Barbara wrote to the Salvation Army mission hospital at Dhariwal where they had an excellent training program. They replied that if the sanatorium would sponsor him and pay his tuition, they would admit him. We agreed on the understanding that Chand would return and work at Jubar.

Tragically, at the last moment Chand declined. He said that he was afraid he might fail and lose face. Despite our pleading, he gave up a wonderful opportunity to help himself.

Births, deaths, weddings, and religious festivals made up the social life. Since almost all weddings were arranged by the parents, generally without consulting their children, they held a particular interest for us.

To attend one *shaddi* or wedding, we hiked to a village two thousand feet down in the valley behind our house. Passing through rocky glades and pine forests, we enjoyed the mewing of peafowl and the chatter of magpies. It was a beautiful walk.

The village consisted of ten small stone houses. We were ushered into the largest where we joined others in a festive but greasy meal. There we met the prospective groom, a strapping young man of twenty-one. His bride-to-be, a child of eight, was busy playing with her friends outside. We wondered about the disparity in age until we were told that she would live at home until she reached puberty and only then would the marriage be consummated. We did not stay for the rest of the ceremony, for that was to take place at two o'clock the following morning, the hour the *pundits* (priests) deemed auspicious.

Although dowry was technically illegal, there was a definite "bride price," and women were occasionally bought and sold.

Sajni, one of our ward aides, was thirteen when she was sold into marriage to a seventy-year-old man. After a few years, her husband tired of her and resold her to a younger man for a better price. Of course he never consulted Sajni.

Once we attended a banquet given by Ver Das. For four hundred rupees (about eighty-eight dollars) he had just bought his second wife, the sister of his first. When we arrived, the two wives were sitting side by side, dressed identically. Neither uttered a word during the meal.

When Narian Das, our very competent operating room orderly, wanted to marry his daughter off, he arranged to have her marry Roop, the oldest son of Santhu, the hospital cook. We were invited, and planned to attend.

The evening before the wedding, Narian and Santhu had a bitter argument, and the marriage was canceled. Having made all the arrangements, bought the food, and paid the pundit, Narian would now to be out a handsome sum, one he could ill afford.

The next morning, we learned that the wedding would still take place. We were delighted that Narian and Santhu had settled their differences, and said so. But, no, they had not. Narian had simply gone elsewhere, and found another family willing and happy to have their son marry his daughter.

We never learned what the principals thought about the arrangement.

Where Is God Not?

At weddings in the Jubar hills, it was the custom to give money to the family of the bride. These gifts were carefully recorded in a ledger. To our surprise, when Narian received a gift of money from Nabi Das, a fellow hospital worker, he returned part of it. Knowing that Narian needed the money, we asked why. He pointed out that when Nabi Das's daughters got married, he would have to reciprocate with an equal gift. Since Narian had but one daughter, and Nabi Das had three, he would be the loser.

Attempts to promote much-needed family planning opened a window to an unexpected aspect of village life. It came about when Sartago became our patient.

Sartago was little more than skin and bones when she was brought to the sanatorium in a dandy. She claimed to be twenty-two years old, but looked more like a scared teenager. She must have been correct about her age, for she was already the mother of three.

Her emaciation and persistent cough suggested tuberculosis, a diagnosis promptly confirmed by x-ray. Although her disease was far advanced, with time and medicine cure was probable, for, unlike most of the patients who came to the sanatorium, she had never been treated. Her germs had not yet developed drug resistance.

To prevent her children from being infected, she was admitted. She improved rapidly, gaining weight and strength. Within a few months she looked like a new person.

From past experience we knew that further pregnancies were inadvisable and suggested that her husband have a vasectomy. To our surprise, he agreed, but said that he would have to discuss it at a family council. He would come back the next day for the operation. We were delighted.

However, local custom intervened.

When he returned the next day he told us that the family had refused. When asked why, he replied,

"Everybody agreed that we do not need more children, and to my having a vasectomy."

"So what is the problem?"

"Well, one of the older men stood up and asked what will happen when Sartago returns, and lives in the village? It will not be pleasant for you when she gets pregnant again."

We had never considered that possibility. We still had much to learn.

Tubal ligation on Sartago was offered as an alternative, but the family refused.

Complicating the problems of family planning was the high infant mortality rate.

Juli, a cheerful middle-aged woman from a nearby village, had been under treatment for several months. One day when we visited her on our daily rounds she started crying.

"What is wrong?" we asked.

"My youngest daughter is getting married tomorrow."

"How old is she?"

"She is fifteen."

This was not surprising, for girls were usually married at puberty. Since Juli had a thirty-four-year-old son, we wondered how many children she had.

"Only four," she answered.

One of the nurses pried further, pointing out that there was a long gap between a thirty-four-year-old son and a fifteen-year-old girl, yet she had only four children. Juli answered, "I thought you meant living children. I had fourteen, but the other ten died."

In addition, there was a deep fear of family planning procedures.

When he started working for us, our cook, Yusuf, had three sons and a daughter. His wife had borne four more children, all of whom had died in infancy. Barbara and I thought that his family was large enough considering his limited earning capacity. Risking our relationship, she suggested that he have a vasectomy, or his wife a tubal ligation.

The former was totally out of the question. He would not have an operation. But one on his wife was acceptable. Reluctantly, she agreed.

When the day for surgery came, Yusuf had second thoughts.

There would be no operation. That was final. We asked why.

"Doctorji,** you know that I am a hill man. When I retire, my wife and I will return to our village in the Garhwal hills. There we will have to work hard. After an operation my wife will no longer be able to carry a *maund* (eighty pounds) on her head."

Without getting into a discussion of why she would have to do such arduous work, we made it clear that she would not be permanently weakened by an operation. He remained adamant.

They had another three children before nature took its course.

The problem of overpopulation plagued us constantly. In our own country, well-meaning friends often criticized our meager efforts to improve health care in the developing world.

As they correctly pointed out, the elimination or reduction in the incidence of communicable and preventable diseases such as smallpox and malaria contributed to overpopulation and they suggested that we should place more emphasis on family planning, an idea we strongly supported. But the problem was not so simple, for only when women could be certain that the children they bore would have a reasonable chance of growing up, would they be willing to limit the size of their families.

This was particularly true in India where society dictated that sons provide for their parents in their old age. In a land where two-thirds of the family income went for food, few earned enough to save for retirement. Daughters were considered to have left their family when they married, and therefore no longer responsible for their own parents. In addition, few jobs offered any pension, and there was no equivalent of social security.

**Ji is an honorific expression, and was often attached at the end of a name or title.

CHAPTER 11

It Takes Two to Have an Argument

CHINA'S INVASION OF TIBET HELPED THE SANATORIUM indirectly.

In the 1950s China invaded Tibet, brutalizing the peaceful populace. Shamefully, the West, including the United States, showed little or no concern. As a result, Tibetans by the thousands fled across the high Himalayan passes into India. Many died, most lost their possessions, all became refugees. They were sent to camps scattered around the country, families often separated. Conditions were crowded and scores developed tuberculosis, a disease to which they had little resistance.

The Central Relief Committee (CRC) in New Delhi, an organization supported by both Christian groups and agencies of the United Nations, selected the Lady Irwin Sanatorium to treat those who came down with the disease. Our sanatorium was the only sanatorium in the mountains that met their criteria—low cost and a willingness to care for patients of all ages.

Like most Americans, we knew little or nothing about Tibet and Tibetans, imagining the latter to be similar to the Chinese in appearance, size, and culture. We soon discovered that they were larger and more muscular, their culture very different and centered on the Dalai Lama. We came to hold them in high regard and learned a little of the hardships they had endured fighting for their lost freedom. Many bore the scars of war.

Where Is God Not?

As was true for our Tibetan patients, this man had walked across the Himalayan Mountains to escape the Chinese invaders.

Besides treating their tuberculosis, the CRC hoped to reha-bilitate and retrain the older patients and educate the children. Unfortunately, we were only partially successful, for Jubar was isolated, and staff difficult to recruit.

The rehabilitation program was under the direction of a Mr. Jones. He was an eccentric European sent from Delhi by the CRC. How they came to employ him, or where he came from we never learned. He taught the women how to use hand-operated sewing machines and the men to make papier-mâché figures. The patterns he used were ugly and useless, and our staff wondered if anyone would ever buy any of them. Thankfully this part of the project did not last long.

Mr. Jones was in India on a long-expired tourist visa. About a year after he came to Jubar the police arrested and deported him. Thereafter the nurses taught both the men and women how to use sewing machines. On discharge from the hospital the CRC gave a machine to each patient who had mastered it.

The school, on the other hand, proved to be much more successful. Our young patients ranged in age from one to twelve. They were lovable and promptly captivated the staff. The younger children were mischievous and thoroughly spoiled by all. The older children were remarkably well-behaved and disciplined.

Many were homeless and had been separated from their parents for years. Others were sent to us from schools that remained open all year, for the children had no homes to go to. One child told us that his mother worked in Mysore, far to the south, his father in Dalhousie, many miles to the west, while his older brother was in school in Darjeeling, thirty-six hours by train to the east. Others told similar tales.

They arrived at the sanatorium with little to their name. So Barbara found a use for the clothes our own children had outgrown.

The rehabilitation program for the Tibetans included teaching them to use sewing machines. In good weather this was done out-of-doors.

Where Is God Not?

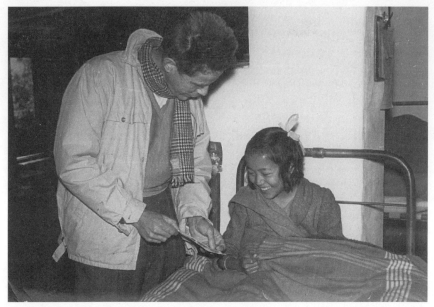

Everybody fell in love with the Tibetan children.

The CRC offered to pay for a trained teacher if we could find one. Unfortunately, there was a nationwide shortage and none were willing to come to an isolated and lonely place like Jubar.

Luckily, one of our Indian patients was studying to be a teacher. Because her family found it difficult to pay for her treatment, we offered to treat her for nothing and give her a small stipend if she would teach the school. She agreed and did a wonderful job, staying with us many months after she could have gone home.

The Tibetans were deeply religious Buddhists; most of them had one or more photographs of the Dalai Lama by their bedside. He was revered, not merely as a messenger of God, but as God incarnate.

It seemed as though every tenth man was a lama or priest. Among them there was a definite pecking order. The ranking lama had numerous pictures of the Dalai Lama on the wall beside his bed. Beneath them on a small table were several tiny bowls of clarified butter. This served as an altar.

The lamas spent long hours reading their holy book. These they copied on strips of thick paper or parchment about fifteen inches long and three or four inches wide. They kept them between two pieces of highly polished wood and wrapped everything together in a cloth.

They showed an amazing artistic talent. One year they painted our Christmas cards for us, using our old ones as models. All the facial features were, naturally, oriental.

They fashioned intricately designed masks out of the clay-like soil and painted them carefully in bright colors. Hoping to take one back home to my sister, I asked them to make one for me. They were delighted. As the masks were fragile, we suggested that they bake them in an oven to harden them before painting.

The reaction was instantaneous. "Of course not, would you put your God into a furnace?"

We received a lesson in justice from them.

We had just driven through the hospital gates when the manager came running to tell us that there had been a fight between two patients.

A Sikh patient, Gurdev Singh, had an argument with Tsering, a Tibetan. For one reason or another, Gurdev picked up a stick and hit Tsering hard on his shin, drawing blood. Concerned lest this escalate into a communal confrontation, I called the resident doctor. He said that the matter had been settled.

I asked him how. He told us that when the incident took place, the other patients had rushed in and separated the combatants. They had taken Gurdev Singh and Tsering to Lobsang, the senior lama. Both combatants agreed to abide by Lobsang's decision.

After questioning the principals, Lobsang told Gurdev Singh, "As you are not of our faith, I shall be lenient with you. I fine you 50 rupees."

Turning to Tsering he added, "If you had started this fight, I would have fined you one hundred rupees. Since you did not, I shall fine you only ten rupees."

The combatants paid readily.

The patients took the money and sent one of their number to Skaktighat, the nearby village. They bought cakes and candy and the ward had a party. A few days later Tsering told us that had they been in Tibet, they would have bought a yakskin full of the local brew and everybody would have gotten drunk.

I asked, "Why was Tsering fined? Was he not an innocent victim?"

The doctor had asked the same question and Lobsang had replied, "When fights take place in Tibet both parties are fined, for it takes two to have an argument."

Our Tibetan patients ate heartily, often preparing their own foods. These held no appeal for us, particularly the tea for which they were famous. This they brewed in a churnlike vessel, adding copious quantities of rancid butter.

Nor did we appreciate one of the ways they preserved meat.

Dorji and her husband, Denzing, had been transferred to our surgical service at Ludhiana from Landour Community Hospital because of a massive wound infection she had developed following an emergency operation. Because her wound was badly infected and gave off a strong odor, we put her in an isolation room adjacent to the ward. Since she spoke nothing but Tibetan, we let her husband stay with her to translate. He also helped care for and feed her.

With repeated dressings, antibiotics and rest, her condition slowly improved and her wound started to heal.

Several days later when we entered her room with the house staff, a revolting odor greeted us. It smelled like rotting meat.

The resident in charge of the ward asked, "How is Dorji doing?"

The intern said, "She is doing very well, her wound is nearly healed."

"Then what is the cause of this smell?"

Looking a bit sheepish, the intern replied, "I don't know— there must be something wrong."

The dressing cart was brought and the bandages removed. The wound was perfectly healed.

But the problem of the odor remained. Finally one of the medical students traced it to a stinking lump in her bedside stand. Denzing was sent for, and asked what the disgusting mass was.

"A leg of goat meat."

"Apparently you do not know that it is rotten and not fit to eat."

Denzing became quite indignant and said, "This meat is only just becoming fit to eat."

CHAPTER 12

Closing Jubar

THE SANATORIUM HAD TO CLOSE.

In the early 1970s the day of the tuberculosis sanatorium was coming to an end. Newer and more potent medicines made ambulatory treatment possible, and as more physicians entered this speciality the government was opening clinics everywhere. Patients no longer needed to be treated far from home.

Finances played a key role, for sanatorium care was expensive. While we struggled to keep expenses down, the cost of food kept increasing, salaries rose, and more and more patients asked to be treated at home. The sanatorium which at best had never more than just broken even, now faced mounting deficits. The government had stopped supporting patients several years earlier and the Central Relief Committee had become our major source of income. But they were having problems of their own and informed us that they would no longer be able to send patients after 1974.

This was particularly unfortunate for the Tibetans. They had been isolated from the rest of the world for centuries and had little resistance to tuberculosis.

Again they were victims of world politics. Some of the support of the Central Relief Committee came from Christian organizations, the rest from agencies of the United Nations. We were told that China strongly objected to Tibetans being classified as refugees, saying that they were free to return home, an obvious impossibility. The United Nations was being pressured to drop their help to the Central Relief Committee.

Having managed the sanatorium for twenty of its forty-five years, we were saddened, for we loved the place and its people. In addition, the staff depended on it for their living. Fortunately, with our help, most of the latter were able to find jobs; the rest, all local farmers, returned to their fields.

We gave the patients summaries of their treatment and their x-rays and referred them to clinics and physicians where they could receive care.

Closing the 120-bed hospital was not easy. We hired trucks, sent the medical equipment to Ludhiana, and auctioned off the rest of the furnishings. The oil barrels in which we had shipped our belongings from America and which we had donated to the sanatorium were especially prized—they could be used as rat-proof containers for storing rice, wheat, and other perishables.

Our last day in Jubar was the saddest. We recalled the warmth with which we had been greeted twenty years earlier, how Bobby had played in the maintenance shop, and how the nurses had taught Carol to wear a sari. Barbara and I and our children had climbed the mountainsides and descended into the valleys nearby. We had fought wildfires and survived droughts. The people had been good, and good to us. We would miss them.

But it was time to move on.

We served tea and simple refreshments to our staff and gave each a small personal memento for their loyal and faithful service. As they worked late into the evening loading trucks, the electricity symbolically failed yet again. By the light of a full moon Barbara finished typing long lists of equipment being sent to Ludhiana.

After one last tearful dinner with the nurses, we got into our packed jeep for our final trip down the mountain. As we started the motor, Sister Taj, our caring charge nurse, and a dear friend, called for to us to wait. She had a present—Brownie, a hopelessly

Where Is God Not?

spoiled cocker spaniel. For the next nine years she was a constant living and loving reminder of a closed chapter in our lives.

As we drove one last time down the mountain, we remembered the thousands of patients, Christian, Muslim, Buddhist, Hindu, Jain, and Sikh, many refugees from wars or revolutions, who had been there. A few had been wealthy, but most poor. Many were cured, others given relief, some were beyond hope when they arrived. All were treated and cared for with love and Christian compassion.

PART TWO
LUDHIANA, INDIA

CHAPTER 13

Ludhiana

LUDHIANA WAS A DYNAMIC EXCITING CITY.

Barbara and I moved there in November 1954 so that I could work at the Christian Medical College. At the same time, we continued to visit the sanatorium every two to three weeks until it closed.

With over a thousand hosiery and woolen mills, Ludhiana was on its way to becoming the industrial capital of the state of Punjab. Many of these mills consisted of a single loom in the center of a small room in which the family lived, slept and played. New factories were springing up every day, producing bicycles, hosiery, sweaters, scooters, sewing machines, lathes, and other items too numerous to count. Much of the industry and the energy to fuel it came from the tens of thousands of refugees from Pakistan scrambling to make a new beginning.

The city lay 190 miles north and slightly west of Delhi on the northern part of the Gangetic plain. It was 710 feet above sea level, and seven miles from the Sutlej River, one of the five rivers from which the Punjab derived its name. Like many towns and cities thereabouts, it sat on a small hill, about ten feet above the surrounding farmland. The latter, in turn, was heavily laced with irrigation canals. Where these were insufficient to satisfy the need for water, there were scores of Persian waterwheels powered by bullocks or haughty camels. In time these were gradually replaced by diesel or electric pumps.

Where Is God Not?

The soil was fertile, but farming had not yet reached its full potential. This was accomplished during the next two decades, when the "green" revolution came to India.

Major highways were paved and reasonably well maintained. Villages were connected by dirt roads, often rendered impassible during the monsoons. Each village was basically a self-contained community, governed by an elected hierarchy of five—the panchayat. The village center, often under an enormous pepul tree, provided a community meeting place. So did the village pond, where women washed their clothes alongside the buffalo and cattle. Family life centered in small courtyards, frequently shared with goats, cattle, buffalo, and the omnipresent pye-dogs. Sweepers and other outcastes lived on the edges of the villages, rarely owning any land, and certainly not socializing with the others.

The climate was generally predictable. Winter began in mid-November and lasted until the middle of March. Temperatures dropped to the thirties, but rarely below freezing. This would not have been uncomfortable had not our buildings been designed for summer. Central heating was unknown, and fuel of all types expensive. The hospital wards, laboratories, and offices were unheated; patients shivered, and so did we.

In March the climate changed, and temperatures began to rise, often touching 90 degrees or more. Koels, birds the size of small crows, announced the arrival of the hot season with their shrill distinctive multiple "khoo" calls, each note higher than the last. When they reached a fever pitch at the seventh or eighth note, they ended abruptly, only to begin again in a few minutes. They earned their more descriptive names of "brain-fever birds."

During April, May, and June the mercury continued its upward spiral, reaching 100 degrees or more almost daily. Recordings of 110 degrees were common, and the thermometer read 118 degrees on occasion. Nights were cooler, averaging 85 degrees or more. When the electricity failed, a regular occurrence, ceiling fans stopped, taking away the slight relief they provided. Blinding dust storms came with the dry season with dust permeating everywhere, coating everything, ruining expensive equipment. The dust storms lessened as more and more land came under cultivation and roads were paved.

In July the monsoon, not overly severe in the Punjab, broke, and temperatures fell to the 80s and 90s. The brown countryside turned green overnight, the rains washed the air clean and, on occasion, the mountains, sixty miles away, could be seen from the rooftops. However, the humidity rose, equaling or surpassing the temperature. August and September were damp and hot.

October and the first half of November were pleasant.

Ludhiana was growing without visible plan. Bazaars were crowded, with signs in four languages: Punjabi, the tongue of the villages, Hindi, the "national" language; Urdu, mostly spoken and read by oldsters, many of whom had come from Pakistan; and English, the lingua franca of the country. Streets were narrow, congested beyond belief with pedestrians, rickshaws, horse-drawn *tongas* (two-wheeled carts), ox carts, buffalo carts, bicycles, trucks, and an occasional automobile. In time, the population quadrupled, easily passing the million mark; tongas disappeared only to be replaced by countless mopeds and scooters. Automobiles multiplied a thousandfold, and innumerable trucks blocked passage for all. Traffic rules may have existed, but the only one that counted was simple—the biggest vehicle got the right of way.

Open sewers ran along the sides of narrow streets with children squatting over them to answer calls of nature. Since the street was also their playground, they were constantly exposed to disease.

The medical college and its hospital, the Brown Memorial Hospital (named after its founder), were situated on the eastern edge of the city. With the exception of a few newly constructed houses for doctors and missionary staff, the college and hospital buildings were old and in a deplorable state.

The institution had embarked on a comprehensive program of modernization and was introducing a new and better curriculum, one that was the equivalent of that in the West. The foundation stone of a new hospital had just been laid, and work was in progress. It was an exciting and challenging time to join the staff.

The hospital had been started in 1881 as a one-room dispensary in the bazaar by a missionary from Scotland, Miss Rose Greenfield.

Where Is God Not?

Started in 1881, the hospital was dedicated to the glory of God.

It grew rapidly, and served as a *zenana* hospital, treating only women and children until the carnage accompanying the partition of India in 1947 forced it to admit men.

In 1894 Dr. Edith Brown, a British missionary, founded what would become the Christian Medical College. Its original objective was to train Christian women to work with missionaries and serve the Muslim women of the area who were unwilling to be examined by male doctors.

Over the years its goals changed, for in 1947 the Muslims fled to Pakistan and the hospital became a general hospital. Soon the institution was training doctors, nurses, and paramedical workers to serve in India, particularly in mission hospitals. The college opened its doors to men students for the first time in 1952.

The college admitted fifty medical students annually. They came from all over India, and competition for admission was intense. Their motivation was sometimes difficult to determine, for some of them applied only because of parental pressure. Fortunately, most of the latter did well and became excellent and caring physicians.

At the time of our arrival, two-thirds of the faculty were missionaries from widely different backgrounds. There were Methodists, Baptists, Anglicans, Presbyterians, Plymouth Brethren, and others of various denominations from England, Scotland, New Zealand, America, Australia, Ireland, and Canada. Others would later come from Germany, Holland, and Switzerland. Over the years a deliberate and highly successful effort was made to train Indian physicians to take their places.

As in all medical colleges in India, classes were taught in English. While easy for the teachers, this was not true for the students. They had been brought up speaking Hindi, Punjabi, Maharathi, Tamil, Malayalam, Bengali, or another of the many languages used throughout the country. They had learned English in school as a foreign language, but now had to cope

Dr. Edith Brown founded the medical college in 1894 to train physicians for India.

with a babel of English accents—the twang of the Australians, the short-clipped tones of the British, the guttural notes of the Germans, and a drawl from Oklahoma. During their first years they struggled greatly, but by the time of their graduation, they had mastered English as well as medicine.

As Americans, we, too, had our linguistic problems, for the English spoken was different from that in our homeland. We soon learned that "water was laid on" meant that there was running water in the house, and when a friend called Barbara "homely," I had to be reassured that he only meant that she was home-loving.

The British influence carried over into the hospital, and was the cause of an unpleasant experience. During our first summer I made a major and nearly fatal clinical misjudgment. I removed the right lung from Bhagwan Das, a very sick patient. The error was not in the operation, but in its timing, for it was June and the thermometer registered 110 degrees in the shade. There was no

Our medical students were from all parts of India and all faiths. Half were women.

air-conditioning in the hospital and, it would have been wise to postpone the surgery until the temperature moderated. The operation had been long and difficult, with the patient in shock much of the time. Postoperatively, Bhagwan Das had been sent to what passed for a recovery room. After reviewing the orders on the chart, I went for a quick lunch. Returning to check on his condition, I was stopped at the entrance by the English nursing superintendent.

She asked, "What can I do for you?"

"I've come to see Bhagwan Das in the recovery room."

"Doctor," she answered, "this is rest time, and doctors are not allowed in the hospital until four o'clock."

"Bhagwan Das is very sick and I have to see him."

"Doctor, you do not seem to understand. The hospital is closed now. Come back at four."

I lost my temper. "I will see any patient of mine anytime I think I should."

As I stormed off towards the recovery room, I heard her say to a friend, "Oh, these Americans!"

Fortunately, Bhagwan Das recovered.

This was not the last time this epithet was used. That same summer Dr. Bill Virgin, then the chief of surgery, had an infected finger and asked me to look after his patients for a few days. The first patient I admitted was Ajit Singh, a farmer from a nearby village. He had fallen off his tractor and had been run over by it. He remained home for two days and only when he was convinced he would die did he agree to be taken to a hospital. When he arrived, he was severely dehydrated and in deep shock. After giving him the appropriate intravenous fluids and medicines, we operated on him.

During the postoperative period Ajit Singh complained of extreme weakness. This was probably the result of a lack of potassium. At the time we had no reliable method of measuring potassium in the blood, yet he needed it desperately and had to be given it intravenously, a procedure that had became routine during my years at Bellevue. In addition, because of the searing heat and the copious quantities of liquids he was losing from his body, we ordered seven liters of intravenous fluids for him, an amount that in later years was not regarded as excessive under similar circumstances.

The hospital pharmacist sought me out. "I think you have made a mistake. That is fourteen bottles of fluids. We never give that much. Don't you mean seven bottles?"

"No. I meant seven liters—fourteen bottles. Ajit Singh has lost more than normal from his stomach tube and in this temperature and with his fever he is sweating a lot."

"Well, all right. But I see you have also ordered potassium intravenously. We have never given that. We have no method of making it."

"I'll tell you how," came my answer.

"But you are not a pharmacist."

He had underestimated my training at Bellevue, for we had been forced to make our own potassium solutions on the wards. I told him how much potassium chloride to add to some of the bottles and assured him that he would not be held responsible for the outcome. Looking skeptical, he reluctantly did what was requested. As I left the pharmacy with my small victory, once again I heard the cry, "Oh, these Americans!"

To everyone's delight and our pharmacist's amazement, the patient made an uneventful recovery.

CHAPTER 14

Where Is God Not?

WHEN WE MOVED TO LUDHIANA WE WERE ASSIGNED A house with room enough around it for Bobby and Carol to play as well as for a small garden.

Our new home was designed for the hot summers. The sole source of heat was a small fireplace of dubious value in the living room. As a result the house was constantly cold in winter.

Chipklies, small yellow-green lizards, scrambled over the inside walls and upside down on the ceilings, dropping dirty souvenirs on the furniture and floors. Although rumored to eat mosquitoes, they seemed to prefer moths and other insects. Termites, called "white ants," built long tunnels of mud up and down the walls in intricate design, feasting on our books and anything made of wood or paper.

The local church was a large cavernous structure, seating more than three hundred, with thick brick walls pierced by long windows. Above these was a row of ventilators near the high ceiling. During the worst of the hot season, worshipers clustered together under three rows of ceiling fans.

Kalvari Church had been founded by Rev. John Lowrie, the first Presbyterian missionary to India. His trip to Ludhiana more than a century earlier was much different from ours.

Where Is God Not?

Rev. Lowrie was one of four missionaries sent to India in 1833 from Pittsburgh, Pennsylvania, by the Western Foreign Missionary Society, a forerunner of the Board of Foreign Missions of the Presbyterian Church. After his missionary years, Lowrie was closely associated with the board.

He was accompanied by his wife and Rev. and Mrs. William Reed on their nine-month voyage from Baltimore to Calcutta. Mrs. Lowrie died in Calcutta. When Rev. Reed became ill, he and his wife boarded ship to return to the United States. On the way home he died and was buried at sea.

Lowrie, the sole survivor of this intrepid band of four, made the trip to Ludhiana, first going up the Ganges by barge, losing much of his luggage on the way, and then switching to overland stage. On November 5, 1834, he finally reached Ludhiana.

Ludhiana had been selected for Lowrie's work because it was the westernmost extent of the British Empire. It also provided access to the people in the mountains as well as those on the plains. Seven miles to the west, across the Sutlej River, lay the empire of the Sikhs under Maharajah Ranjit Singh.

In anticipation of Rev. Lowrie's arrival, the local British political agent, Captain John Wade, had founded a school. This he turned over to Lowrie although the latter expressed no desire to be involved in education. Part of this school later became the St. Thomas School, the school that Barbara managed for eleven years.

Maharajah Ranjit Singh was interested in meeting Lowrie and having him start a school for his children and those of his courtiers. He sent a troop of ten horsemen and an elephant to fetch Lowrie. The school never materialized when Lowrie insisted that were he to accept such an offer he would teach the Bible, a condition unacceptable to the maharajah.

Ranjit Singh and Lowrie discussed many things including theology. Ranjit Singh asked Lowrie many questions, among them what would happen to those who broke God's commandments and how he could worship God if he did not know where God was.

Finally Ranjit Singh asked, "Where is God?"

To this Lowrie is said to have answered, "Where is God not?" an answer that greatly impressed the maharajah.

Lowrie returned to Ludhiana with many gifts including a horse. These he sold and turned the proceeds over to his missionary society to Ranjit Singh's bewilderment.

It was in this church that we worshiped for the next thirty-two years and in which I served as an elder.

Lost

"WHERE'S BOBBY?" BARBARA CALLED.

"Isn't he with you?" I answered.

"No, he's not," she replied, anxiety creeping into her voice.

Barbara and I had gone shopping in Chaura Bazaar. Since we had never been there, Dr. Dick Fox, a staff physician from England, had volunteered to accompany us. Our son was three years old and lost.

Chaura Bazaar, meaning wide market, which it was not, was the heart of the shopping district in Ludhiana. Crowded with rich and poor alike, city dwellers, farmers, laborers, young and old, mendicants and beggars, it throbbed with activity. Stores lined the street, with vendors vying for customers. They shouted to the crowds, displaying their wares, ranging from exquisite silk saris to brass pots. Most of the shoppers were on foot, a few rode bicycles, others came on bicycle-rickshaws or horse-drawn tongas, and an occasional brave or foolhardy person drove a car through the crowd, honking furiously.

Barbara and I had gone our separate ways. Bobby and Carol were to go with Dick and Barbara, while I went off to buy a pair of shoes. We planned to meet in half an hour at our Land Rover. When I returned, Barbara, Carol, and Dick were already there, but Bobby was nowhere to be found. Barbara thought that he had gone with me; I, that he had gone with her. While Barbara and Carol waited, Dick and I went searching.

We returned empty-handed. Everybody had seen Bobby, but no two persons could agree where he had gone. There were more rumors than flies. He had been taken to the Christian Medical College, to the government hospital, to the police station, and so on. We began to panic, for newspapers had recently reported several incidents of boys of his age being kidnapped from that bazaar. They were then sold in other parts of the country to professional beggars or to farmers to be used as laborers.

After what seemed a lifetime, an elderly gentleman called out to us and asked why we were going around asking questions. We told him our son was lost. He said, don't worry, he had found Bobby wandering about. Since Bobby said he knew his way home, the shopkeeper had turned him over to his servant to take him there. This was odd, for Bobby had never been to the bazaar.

Chaura Bazaar was the main shopping area in Ludhiana. Many of the signs are in English.

Where Is God Not?

The gentleman reassured us, saying that his servant had been in his employ for twenty-five years and was completely trustworthy.

After a long and futile hour and a half, we returned to the medical college only to find that Bobby was already there, entertaining medical students in Dr. Scovel's house. One of the hospital workers had met the servant in the bazaar and spoken to him in English. Bobby had wrapped his arms around him and refused to let go, so the worker had taken him back to the medical college.

A few days later when we went to Jubar, Bobby announced that his parents had gotten lost.

We thanked God for his mercy.

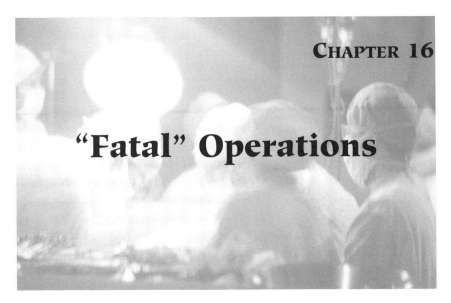

CHAPTER 16

"Fatal" Operations

THE LIGHTS WENT OUT.

We were doing the first major lung operation in Ludhiana and had just reached the point where we could not stop. Without light we could not go on.

Seven weeks after we had arrived in India I had sent two patients, Radha Krishna and Ivy Saphir, from Jubar to Ludhiana. Neither had responded adequately to medical treatment and both needed to have parts of their diseased lungs removed. Such surgery had not yet been done at Ludhiana.

Before going to India, I had stressed that lung surgery should not be done without a qualified anesthetist. Since there was none on the staff, Dr. Snow had sent a senior doctor to a neighboring medical college to learn the necessary skills. She returned fully convinced that she could not give the type of anesthesia needed.

Fortunately, Dr. Ronald Garst, an orthopedic surgeon, had arrived a month after us. He had given anesthesia on occasion, and offered to try. The two of us discussed at length what anesthesia to use, and other details. We would use ether. Having no respirator, Dr. Garst would breathe for the patient by squeezing on a bag connected to the anesthetic machine.

Next we met with the operating room staff to discuss the various steps of the operation and the instruments we would use, many of which were new to them. They were eager for this challenge.

Where Is God Not?

Operations on the lungs require strong continuous suction during the postoperative period. There was no machine available that even closely met our requirements. However, in the storeroom there was an old Wangensteen suction apparatus. Wangensteen suctions were never designed for lung surgery. They used four large bottles, two at a time being full of water which ran into the two empty ones, creating mild suction. The apparatus containing the bottles had to be turned over when the bottles on top were empty.

The only Wangensteen apparatus in the hospital was broken and had been discarded. We repaired it and tested it. Although it leaked continuously, it worked. It would have to do.

Radha Krishna's operation was scheduled for a Tuesday.

Monday evening was the time set aside for the weekly staff prayer meeting, and many were the prayers said for him. We were to need them.

The great day dawned brightly. However, during breakfast the electricity went off, not to return until after lunch. After praying with Radha Krishna and the staff, we made a belated start at three that afternoon. All went as planned for the first hour. Just after passing the point where we could not turn back, the power again failed. We were operating deep inside the chest, dissecting and handling blood vessels the size of one's little finger and could see nothing. It was impossible to continue without light and equally impossible to quit. The hospital had no emergency generator.

We sent for flashlights but these proved inadequate.

My assistant, Dr. William Virgin, an orthopedic surgeon from Canada, remembered that he had a slide projector at home that ran off a car battery. He sent for it and when it arrived a young doctor perched himself on a high stool and directed the light over our shoulders into the gaping wound while we tried to keep out of the way of the beam. Three traumatic and emotional hours later the operation was over. The electricity immediately returned.

I asked Dr. Virgin why his slide projector ran off a battery.

"Forrest, you know that I like to go to the villages and preach the Gospel. Most villages have no electricity and with this projector I can show slides when I am there."

I immediately became a staunch supporter of village evangelism.

Postoperatively, Radha Krishna was put in a private room, with a ward aide to turn the Wangensteen suction bottles over when necessary. The apparatus continued to leak and the room soon became a lake. Fortunately it did its job satisfactorily.

God is good, and Radha Krishna recovered uneventfully.

Ivy Saphir was scheduled for surgery the next day. As a staff nurse, she was well aware of the problems of the previous day. However, she showed great faith and outwardly seemed calm. Because of our earlier problems, Dr. Snow drove her car, a tiny Fiat, into the hospital and parked it next to the operating room. Two wires ran from its generator to an automobile headlight inside, a precaution that proved unnecessary.

Dr. Snow agreed to buy an emergency generator when funds could be found. Meanwhile, if we were not to lose the momentum generated by this auspicious start, we had to continue with our program.

A few months later while we were doing a simple operation on Sunder Das, the electricity began to go off and on sporadically. Finally it quit for good, and we were forced to abandon the procedure. I lost my temper, for Sunder Das would now have to undergo a second painful and unnecessary operation.

Storming out of the operating room I went to Dr. Snow's office.

"I've had it. We can never expect to do chest surgery this way. The electricity is totally unreliable, and we'll have a death in the operation room someday. Sunder Das now has to have another and completely unnecessary operation."

Dr. Snow answered, "Calm down. Lets see if we can do something about it. Is Sunder Das a patient we are treating for the Ludhiana Municipal Tuberculosis Clinic?"

"Yes."

"Then the municipality must help us. Take my car and driver and go see Mr. Isa Das."

Mr. Isa Das was the District Commissioner, the highest official in the local government. It was he who had asked us to treat these patients.

Borrowing Dr. Snow's Fiat, I went off to the municipal offices only to find them closed for a minor government holiday. This made me even more angry, for while we were working for the city, their government was enjoying a day off.

We drove across town to Mr. Isa Das's home. He was busy dictating letters, sitting outside in his garden with an electric fan revolving slowly overhead. The thought that he had electricity in his home for his comfort while we had none in the hospital for our patients was too much. I began to berate the government.

"Sit down," he ordered, "have some tea, then we will discuss the situation."

After tea, when my temper had moderated, he asked what the problem was.

"The electrical supply to the hospital is unreliable. It goes off and on without warning. Someday we will have a disaster as a result. It is not safe to operate under these conditions. This morning it happened again and we had to stop in the middle of an operation. Fortunately, the patient survived, but will have to have another operation."

"I'll see what I can do. Trust me."

Several days later I received a copy of his letter to the regional supervisor of the Electricity Board. His final sentence was clear, "Make certain that the hospital has electricity whenever Dr. Eggleston does any of his fatal operations."

I hoped that this was a typographical error, not a measure of his confidence. However, we continued to have problems until we got our own generator.

CHAPTER 17

See One, Help One, Do One

"MR. SINGH, WHAT DOES THE BLOOD EXAMINATION SHOW?" I asked.

"None was done, sir."

"What does the urinalysis show?"

"None was done, sir."

I was talking to fourth-year medical students on the wards. Dr. Snow had asked me to help teach general surgery while I was developing chest surgery. This was enjoyable but difficult, as another doctor took care of the patients upon whom I taught. The two of us often disagreed about their treatment.

I discussed this problem with Dr. Snow and told her I wanted to limit myself to chest surgery. To my surprise, she asked if I would take charge of the Department of Surgery as the current head was leaving that summer.

I was hesitant, for increasing numbers of patients were coming for chest surgery and we had ambitious plans for the future. Proof that our work was becoming known came from a letter addressed (in Hindi):

"To the American Doctor
Who does Tuberculosis Operations
Ludhiana."

In addition, I felt that I was too young for such an appointment, being but a brash thirty-four. However, I did promise to consider it.

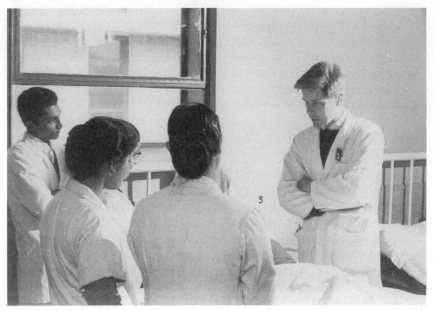

Doing what I liked most—teaching.

That evening Barbara and I discussed Dr. Snow's request in great detail. The opportunity to develop a major department in a way new to India was an exciting challenge. But my experience as a teacher was limited and that as an administrator untested. I could recall only one head of a surgical department in America who had been appointed at a similar age. It suddenly occurred to me that there was no one else on the staff with the qualifications required by the Punjab University to which the college was affiliated. That might have been the reason for Dr. Snow's offer, not a very flattering thought.

A few days later I did agree and Dr. Snow suggested that the change be made the first of October 1955.

The medical college was in the process of changing its entire curriculum. It had been a licentiate school; it was now becoming a degree medical college. Licentiate schools had a four-year course of study; degree colleges required four and a half years followed by a compulsory internship. In addition, the course content of the latter was considerably more extensive.

Obtaining a copy of the university syllabus, Barbara and I went on "vacation" to Jubar to spend the summer preparing lectures and programs for the students who were to be our unknowing but trusting guinea pigs.

At the end of September we returned to Ludhiana full of energy and eager to start the new program. The entire surgical staff consisted of one surgical resident, two house doctors (interns in American parlance), a doctor who ran the surgical OPD, two well-qualified orthopedic surgeons, and me.

There were only eight patients on the surgical service who did not have either orthopedic or chest problems. By any reasonable criterion we should have had at least sixty patients to provide the students an opportunity to study a wide variety of diseases.

To add to my woes, all eight patients had conditions usually treated by urologists, plastic surgeons or neurosurgeons, of whom there were none. I rapidly learned the meaning of the term "general surgery." In India it included everything. The library became my refuge, and I studied operative procedures that I had never even seen. We depended more than ever on prayer and the innate ability of patients to survive. By the grace of God, they usually did.

These changes also resulted in the indefinite postponement of plans to establish a good thoracic surgical service. While this was disappointing, I could now develop a general surgical residency program instead. This would benefit John Vettath, our only surgical resident. He had been doing well in our chest program, but had little training in general surgery.

Surgery in India followed what we understood was a British pattern, with all but the simplest operations being carried out by senior surgeons. At Ludhiana these had been missionaries from the United Kingdom. Results were good, but the Indian staff had not been trained.

At the time when Dr. Virgin had asked me to cover the surgical service when his finger was infected, a patient needing a very simple operation was admitted. In the operating room I handed the scalpel to the young lady doctor who was to assist me and told her to start and I would help her. Such a thing had not happened before, and it was soon apparent that she had not even been taught how to tie surgical knots.

This had to change.

Dr. Snow knew how strongly I felt about this, for from the first time we met, I badgered her repeatedly to find someone to train. Finally, late in August 1954, she told me that she had found a doctor who would like to be a chest surgeon. He would join the institution on the first of October.

John Vettath had less operative experience than I had anticipated. When John looked at me (for I was but five years his senior), and I learned of his inexperience, we almost parted company. Probably both of us thought that neither would do better, and we agreed to give it a try. It was to be the beginning of a friendship that lasted through the years.

John was eager and more than willing to work. During his first three months he learned how to care for our patients before and after surgery and how to help me in the operating room. Soon he was on the way to becoming an excellent surgical assistant. When he was finally ready to do an operation himself, I selected a relatively simple procedure with which he was familiar and assisted him.

Some of the senior faculty questioned the wisdom of my letting John do the operation. They claimed that it was dangerous and irresponsible, and that I was risking the patient's life. The younger and more progressive members of the faculty, particularly Dr. Ron Garst, were all on my side. Once more, Dr. Snow supported me.

When the governing body of the institution met a few months later, one of its members criticized me strongly. She told me, "Mission hospitals do not need the fancy specialists you are training. We shall never need them."

A few years later the same doctor wanted to take a long-overdue vacation and asked us to send a surgeon to her hospital for a few weeks. To her horror, we sent a second-year surgical resident. Nevertheless she did take her vacation, and the resident did an excellent job. After that she was one of my staunchest supporters.

Our surgical house staff in the mid-1960s.

Because the house staff were more involved and interested, patients rapidly increased in numbers, for they got better and more personalized care. We constantly emphasized the need to treat patients as individuals, not merely as medical problems. We insisted that each patient be called by name, and that everybody, students and house staff alike, know where they came from and what their occupations were. I remembered the advice my father had given me—"You do not treat diseases, you treat patients with diseases."

By the time we retired, more than one hundred surgeons had been trained in the program. Some stayed at Ludhiana to staff the surgical department, scores left to work in or run mission hospitals. Others went into private practice, a few went abroad.

Our residency program quickly attracted attention, particularly among recent graduates, for CMC and only CMC offered "hands on" training in surgery. It was founded on the American system of "see one, help one, do one." Despite our insistence on four years of training instead of the three the other medical colleges required, we always had many more applications than we could handle.

We were accused by members of other departments of making residents work too hard and of our program being too long. But those who completed it told us that they wished they could have stayed longer. The residency program was new to India, and drew numerous comments from visitors. Physicians who had been trained in this system were all in favor of it.

However, one surgeon from Ireland was openly critical of it. He asked, "Don't you find that you are not as skillful a surgeon as you would be if you did more of the operations yourself instead of having the residents do them?"

Possibly he was correct, for by then the majority of operations were done by our residents. Senior surgeons assisted, and operated only on the sickest patients or under special circumstances. But when he learned of the many surgeons who had been trained in Ludhiana and had gone on to establish their own surgical services in other mission hospitals, he understood what we were doing and agreed with us.

CHAPTER 18

You Choose

POTASSIUM CAN KILL OR IT CAN CURE.

Essential to life, its lack makes a patient weak and threatens life. An excess is fatal.

Although we knew that it was dangerous, we had been giving potassium to patients without being able to measure it. So far many patients had benefitted and there had been no complications. But we realized that we must get a flame photometer, the instrument used to measure it.

Buying one was out of the question, for they were expensive and funds were not merely limited, they were nonexistent. Fortunately, my surgical training had included a year at New York City's Presbyterian Hospital where the surgeons had been pioneers in the administration of potassium and their staff were skilled in the use of flame photometers.

On our first furlough in 1959 we decided to try and find a used one. I visited friends at Presbyterian and explained my problem. They told me of an old instrument that was no longer used, one on which much of the early research work had been done. It was now considered obsolete.

It would have to do. Indeed, there was no choice.

As the instrument was very large, we arranged to have all but the most sensitive part, a delicate galvanometer, shipped to

Ludhiana by sea. On our eight-thousand mile flight back to India, the Eggleston family took turns carrying the galvanometer on their laps.

When we reassembled the apparatus some four months later, a problem arose. The instrument had been designed to burn propane gas, an item then unavailable in India.

What could we use instead? Someone suggested acetylene. This was easily obtained, as was the oxygen needed to go with it. Soon two large cylinders appeared in the surgical laboratory. However, the burner was designed for propane and refused to work with acetylene. We could find no way to adapt it.

Next we tried gasoline. Eventually this did work, but not until we completely rebuilt the burner. We pumped air through gasoline creating a vapor into which we could add our specimen and then inject it into the burner. We lived in constant fear that the whole apparatus would explode, so we buried the bottles containing gasoline and the vaporizer in large cans filled with sand.

To our delight, we now had a steady flame into which our samples could be introduced and potassium measured accurately. It had taken us a full year, one of extreme frustration, but the monster had been tamed. We now had a flame photometer that worked, albeit temperamentally. It was the only one in North India.

This was the beginning of our scavenging for medical supplies. We were astounded by the vast quantities of medical equipment and medicines that were wasted in our own country when there were such desperate needs abroad.

On that first furlough we collected drug samples. We organized a network of doctors, nurses, and hospitals which sent them to us. Our living room became a sorting room, our children and their friends helping open and pack the medicines. It was hard work, but rewarding.

A year after our return to Ludhiana, representatives of the Rockefeller Foundation visited the institution. When they came to the surgical department, there were only two small rooms for laboratory and experimental work. In one was the flame photometer, in the other a newly acquired spirometer and other apparatus for measuring lung functions. Some of this had been donated by Dr. Andre Cournand whom I had known when working at Bellevue and who had recently been awarded the Nobel Prize.

The Rockefeller visitors wanted to see what research we were doing. We told them that we were establishing normal values for lung functions in the Indian population as we had already proved that Western standards did not apply. One of the visitors commented that our equipment was primitive and difficult to work with. We agreed, but when we showed him that the results were valid, he admitted that the work was accurate.

That evening, we learned that the Rockefeller Foundation would give us a ten thousand dollar grant. This was the start of a program of planned development of a surgical research laboratory, one that resulted in dramatic improvements in patient care and ultimately led to open-heart surgery.

Although the grant from the Rockefeller Foundation combined with generous gifts from friends at home helped us buy essential equipment, there were always shortages. This was dramatically brought home one day.

The telephone rang. "Please come to the recovery room immediately."

When I arrived, Dr. Singh, one of our surgical residents, met me and said, "Dr. Eggleston, please examine my patient. I think he needs a respirator."

We examined the patient together. He was right, and I told him to put his patient on a respirator. Turning to leave, another resident, Dr. Jasbir, stopped me and asked me to see another patient. So again, we reviewed the situation and examined the patient. She also thought that her patient needed a respirator. I agreed, and told her so.

For a second time I started to leave, when both residents stopped me.

"Sir, we have only one respirator—which patient should get it? You choose."

Where Is God Not?

It was a difficult choice.

Shortages occurred because of strikes at factories, the inability of local suppliers to keep adequate stocks, and restrictions on imports. One difficult summer we were without any medicines for pain. Our surgical patients showed a surprising but necessary fortitude, but then they had no choice.

A few years later, x-ray films disappeared from the market. We decreased the frequency with which we took x-rays, hoarding our precious stock, and depended on the less reliable use of fluoroscopy. Did patients suffer medically? Possibly, but we will never know.

Through the kindness of a friend in America, we received a supply of disposable plastic oxygen masks. We could not afford the luxury of discarding them after but one use, so we sterilized them repeatedly until they wore out. Some lasted years.

When we first arrived in India, operations were done in an old hospital due to be replaced. The buildings were well over fifty years old and in poor repair. From our point of view, the major deficiencies were in the operating room suite.

This consisted of but two operating rooms. The first, large and cavernous, allowed two surgical teams to operate at the same time. Its north side was glassed in, painted at the bottom. This provided some light when the power failed. On the south wall there were ventilators near the ceiling, which opened above the roof of the adjacent building which was surfaced with mud mixed with cow dung. During the hot summer months when the ventilators were open, dust drifted into our "sterile" environment. Not only did it seep into the operating room, so did flies. It was not unusual to kill one or two of them before starting surgery in the morning.

Across the hall was a second and smaller room. Its ceiling was poorly finished, and flakes of plaster occasionally fell into open wounds.

Neither room was air-conditioned. During the worst of the summer heat, fans blew air over large blocks of ice, providing

The entrance of the first part of the new hospital, opened in 1957.

minimal relief. Under the hot operating lights we sweated profusely, and sometimes changed our surgical gowns two or three times during a single operation. While discomforting for us, more serious was the break in sterile technic, for bacteria easily passed through sweat-soaked drapes. Why our infection rate was not higher was a mystery.

Equally serious was the problem of heat stroke. During our first June at Ludhiana, a young child died of this after a long and complicated operation. After that, until the first phase of the new hospital was completed, whenever possible we postponed lengthy operations during the hot season.

In the spring of 1957 the first phase of a new hospital was opened. The new operating and recovery rooms were a delight. In addition to being air-conditioned and better equipped, the new rooms now had a standby generator available at a moment's notice. At first the air conditioning was set to keep the temperature at 72 degrees. As summer wore on, when the temperatures outside hovered at 100 degrees or more, the sudden drop in temperature when coming in from out-of-doors was very uncomfortable, and the temperature of the operating room was raised.

The adjacent recovery room was designed for eight patients. As work increased, beds were moved closer and closer together, sometimes doubling the number of patients. It was probably the first recovery room of its kind in North India, and certainly one of the best.

They Will Kill Me

THE RING OF THE TELEPHONE JOLTED ME OUT OF A DEEP sleep.

"Dr. Eggleston, a patient with a stab wound has just been admitted and wants to be your private patient. Please come."

All senior doctors had "private" patients. The term "private" only meant that a senior doctor would carry out the care personally and that the patient would have a private room. They paid more, the income going to the hospital. It helped to pay for the care of the poor.

Two days earlier Hardas Singh had had a fight in his village and was stabbed in the abdomen. He was taken to the local hospital and a bandage applied. There he lay in his bed with no other treatment, his condition gradually worsening. Finally, his doctor, Atam Prakash, brought him to Ludhiana.

Hardas Singh was very sick with a fever of 105 degrees and in shock. His abdomen had an open wound from which a loop of his intestines protruded. He needed surgery urgently.

So we began our usual routine—ice packs to lower his fever, intravenous fluids, antibiotics, and so forth. The family was more than willing to give blood, and, to our surprise, so was Dr. Atam Prakash.

Hardas Singh had generalized peritonitis, and a very stormy and difficult time after surgery. Not surprisingly, he developed a severe wound infection. To the family he appeared to be getting worse, and likely to die.

Dr. Atam Prakash asked to see me privately. He said, "If Hardas Singh needs any special medicine, get it and I will pay for it, but at all costs Hardas Singh must get well."

"We are doing everything possible. I think that he will get well once we get his infection under control. I expect him to live."

Dr. Atam Prakash was not satisfied. "My life is at stake,"

I corrected him, "It is Hardas Singh's life that is at stake."

Atam Prakash interrupted, "You do not know the whole story. I run the hospital in the village where Hardas Singh was stabbed. I am the only doctor in the area and an ophthalmologist. I have never treated a stab wound before and did nothing when I should have. The family has promised to kill me if he dies."

Hardas Singh did live, but there was little doubt that had Hardas Singh died, Atam Prakash would have been our next patient.

Medical practice was very different from that in New York. Patients delayed coming to the hospital, so that their diseases were more advanced and, tragically, often beyond cure.

Financial constraints influenced treatment. Because the cost of a single x-ray or a laboratory test might be more than a week's salary, we ordered as few as possible and instead relied on careful medical histories, physical examinations, and clinical judgment. When we compared our results with those published in medical journals from the West, there was little or no difference in comparable cases.

Emotionally difficult were the unnecessary deaths from easily preventable diseases. Tetanus and typhoid fever ranked near the top of the list. Tetanus was common and frequently fatal, for routine immunization was in its infancy. Mothers and infants died by the score from abortions and deliveries done in villages under unsanitary conditions. Injections given improperly by careless or unqualified medical personnel were sometimes followed by severe infections or even tetanus. Insufficient medical and nursing staff and equipment made the care of these desperately ill patients difficult.

Patients with typhoid fever were usually in their late teens, twenties, or early thirties. Nearly all were poor, for the disease was associated with lack of sanitation. Surgeons treated only those with complications, the most common being perforation of the bowel. The patients arrived in a desperate state, having had generalized peritonitis an average of four days. They needed massive volumes of intravenous fluids for resuscitation, and emergency surgery. Postoperative care was prolonged, difficult, and expensive. Mortality was high, and complications the rule.

One sad summer three children, fourteen, fifteen, and sixteen years old lay side by side in our recovery room, each with peritonitis from typhoid perforations that had occurred from four to six days earlier. All had been treated in other hospitals before being referred to us. One died Tuesday, one Wednesday, one Thursday.

I wept.

We worked hard on this problem, and were rewarded by seeing the mortality rate drop in half.

India was a man's world.

Rajender Kaur came to the outpatient department because of abdominal pain. After examining her and seeing her x-rays, it was obvious that she had stones in her gallbladder and needed surgery. We spent considerable time explaining the problem to her, and the need for an operation. When we asked her if she understood what we had told her, she said, "You will have to consult my husband."

We called him and had to repeat everything. Without saying a word to his wife, he agreed.

Such episodes were repeated daily. Soon we learned to have the husband or a male member of the family present when talking with a female patient. It was usually the man who signed the operative permit.

Where Is God Not?

Occasionally a husband refused permission for a much-needed operation on his wife, despite her being willing to have it. Arguments arose when the patient had a potentially curable cancer. Generally, but not always, we prevailed. When the husband said "no," the wife went home. Sometimes they returned months later, the husband now willing and eager for the operation, the patient now beyond cure.

A few older women were reluctant to go home once they were well. It was hard to understand why, until we realized how difficult their lives were. Living in a male-dominated society, their role in life was one of subservience, and, unless they were getting married or having babies, they were rarely the center of attention. But in the hospital they were, and they enjoyed their new importance. They wanted to make it last as long as possible.

A few families and friends donated blood willingly when transfusions were necessary, but these were in the minority. Late one night Lal Chand brought his six-month-old son to the hospital because the child was having increasing difficulty in breathing. After examination, it was clear that the child needed an operation soon. However, the child was anemic and would probably require blood during his surgery.

Lal Chand refused to donate, saying that he had "blood pressure." A surgical resident checked him and assured him that his blood pressure was quite normal. Next he felt "too weak." He was thoroughly examined and found in excellent health. Finally he said that he would buy blood, something that we discouraged since most professional donors were beggars or rickshaw pullers who were themselves anemic and often had malaria. Hospital policy dictated that relatives or friends donate whenever possible. When no family members were available and a patient's life hung in the balance, medical students and staff donated generously, some of them many times. However, in this instance the father could easily donate.

Lal Chand refused and took his son home with him.

The next morning, he returned. His son was worse. Would we reconsider, he asked? We remained adamant. So he rolled up his sleeve and donated. The necessary surgery was done, using the blood, and his son recovered.

After that, whenever we met him, he would tell us how grateful he was, and boast to all within hearing how he had given blood willingly.

Besides India's cultural differences in medical practice, diseases that had been but briefly mentioned during my training became everyday problems. In addition to typhoid fever and tetanus, I became acquainted with hydatid cysts, leprosy, and amebiasis, the latter personally as well as professionally. I learned that the omnipresent tuberculosis could mimic many other conditions. My medical perspective was changing.

Too often patients delayed coming to the hospital, waiting days, weeks, or even months. They arrived in advanced stages of disease. While diagnosis was easy, treatment was more difficult and often only palliation was possible. Fortunately, opium was readily available in the villages, and those who were dying of cancer were sometimes advised to return home and take it.

The long delays were discouraging. We spent countless hours educating the public on the need for early diagnosis, particularly of cancer. Our faculty spoke at local Rotary and Lions clubs. To help us, these clubs prepared and distributed posters and hand-bills in Punjabi, Hindi, Urdu, and English. Our surgical residents gave talks to patients and relatives as they waited in the OPD. As more and more patients were cured, the public became better educated, and started to come to the hospital earlier.

Some diseases carried a stigma that families tried to hide. Sheena, a vivacious seventeen-year-old college student from Jullunder (now renamed Jalandhar), was brought to the hospital by her parents. She was found to have advanced but curable tuberculosis. When we told her parents this, they asked if we would treat her, as they had lost confidence in their own physician. We agreed, and started back to talk with her.

Immediately her father blocked our way, saying, "Don't tell her what she has."

I explained that we had to talk to her to get her cooperation, for treatment might take a year or more. Her father said that we

Where Is God Not?

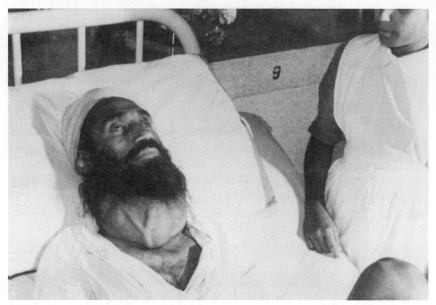

This patient waited many years before seeking medical treatment. He recovered uneventfully following surgery.

could tell her that, but not the diagnosis.

Previous unfortunate experiences had taught us that tubercular patients often stopped taking their medicines once they began to feel better. It was essential that Sheena understand what the diagnosis was, and what the treatment would be. We told the family this, but they were adamant.

So I asked the nurse to return their consultation fee, for we would not treat her under these conditions. The family pleaded with us to reconsider but we refused.

Sheena's family, and there were at least ten of them present, caucused. After much debate and argument, they agreed to abide by our decision—we could do what we thought best.

I returned to Sheena. "You have tuberculosis. Fortunately, it is curable."

She broke into tears.

I thought that maybe the family had been right. So I went on. "When I was young, I had tuberculosis and was cured.

98

There is no doubt in my mind that if you follow our orders you too will be cured."

She stopped crying, she looked at me and said, "Thank you, doctor. I knew I had something serious. Because my family would not tell me, I thought it was cancer, and that I would die soon."

After that, getting her cooperation was easy and she made a complete recovery.

Family hierarchy played a major role in patient care.

Mr. Ram Suran, a wealthy sixty-two-year-old businessman, noticed that he could no longer pass urine freely. We confirmed the diagnosis that he had been dreading—he had an enlarged prostate. He would need an operation, if not now, sometime soon. He begged to postpone it as long as possible. We warned him about possible consequences and he went on his way.

Two months later, he returned to the emergency room, unable to pass urine at all. A catheter was inserted and he was admitted. After completing the necessary tests, we scheduled him for operation the following Wednesday. He said, no, that was too soon. Although greatly troubled by his catheter, he wanted to wait.

When asked why, his reply was simple, "I don't have permission."

He went on to explain, "I'll have to wait until my older brother comes from Calcutta. He is the head of our family and he will make the decision."

His brother was two years older.

We waited. As expected, his brother approved, and Ram Suran soon went home well.

Gurus, or religious leaders, influenced patient decisions.

Om Prakash and his wife Santosh came to see us together. He had a moderately large stone in his left kidney, she a gallbladder full of small stones. They wanted a private room and me to do the surgery, but were concerned about the expense. I suggested that we could do their operations the same day, and they would save by sharing a room. They welcomed the idea, and a date was set.

Suddenly Om Prakash demurred. They would have to get permission from their guru—Sai Baba.

Sai Baba was a famous "God Man" who was said to be able to tell the past and predict the future. His devotees numbered in the thousands.

Three weeks later Om Prakash and Santosh returned—Sai Baba had given permission for me to operate. So they were scheduled for the next day.

But Om Prakash had changed his mind about having both operations done at the same time. Santosh would go first and only if that were successful, would he have surgery. Both recovered uneventfully.

A few patients refused treatment if they thought it might hurt other members of their family. Such was Raj Rani.

She had a hard lump in her breast, an obvious cancer. Although rather large, it was operable. However, she was severely anemic, and it was not safe to operate without blood available. Since she had three strapping sons, all in excellent health, there should have been no problem. When approached, they were, as usual, "too weak." All of them were stronger than any of us, but, no, they would not give blood. When told that their mother's life was in the balance, they reluctantly agreed, and we made the necessary arrangements.

When Raj Rani heard of this, she slipped out of the hospital at night rather than let her sons donate blood.

We never saw her again.

Seasonal factors also created problems.

Balbir Singh was referred to us from another hospital after his chest had been crushed in a near-fatal tractor accident. He had developed a diaphragmatic hernia, a condition that should be corrected as soon as possible. As he had no symptoms, he was understandably reluctant, and asked to postpone the operation. We were loath to agree as this hernia posed a very real danger. This was explained to him and his brother, Onkar Singh.

But the harvest season had started, and all available help was needed in the fields. The brothers felt that if they knew the danger signs they could go home and return at the first hint of trouble. So against our advice, and after once again being warned of possible complications, the brothers went home.

We did not see the family again for the next six months. When we met Onkar Singh again, I asked, "How is Balbir?"

"Oh, he is dead."

"What happened?"

Onkar Singh answered, "Doctor, he developed the exact symptoms you warned us about."

"Then why didn't you bring him back? We told you not to delay."

"Doctor, we wanted to, but it happened during the monsoon, and our village was completely isolated for the four days it took him to die."

A few families simply did not care.

Nishi was twenty-five years old when her husband abandoned her and her newborn baby. Shortly thereafter, she was admitted late one night with generalized peritonitis, the result of a perforation of her bowel from tuberculosis. Her operation was followed by a prolonged and difficult convalescence. Finally she was able to go home but had a wound that needed frequent dressings. Her brother promised he would give her the necessary medicines and arrange for her care.

Three months later her brother carried her into our outpatient department. She had lost nearly half her weight and her wound was discharging great quantities of foul pus. After taking her home, her brother had rarely done any dressings, and gave her medicines only when it suited him.

She needed to be in the hospital.

Her brother refused, and said he did not care what happened to her. She and her child were burdens to him. The nurses and surgical residents argued with him unsuccessfully. We offered free treatment but he refused it. Nishi cried out to be admitted. Finally her brother picked her up and took her away almost certainly to die.

CHAPTER 20

Kali's Agent

KALI CAME TO TOWN.

Kali, the destroyer, was one of the countless gods of the Hindu pantheon. She was one of several personifications of Parvati, Shiva's consort. Kali, meaning black, was portrayed as such, often with a terrifying expression. She wore a garland of human heads and a skirt of severed limbs. Paradoxically, she was also depicted as a goddess of tender love and even of healing.

Her vast temple complex in Calcutta swarmed with hordes of worshipers and scores of filthy beggars. To visit the various temples, one had to thread one's way gingerly and barefoot through piles of dung left by the numerous dogs and goats that roamed at will. Several temples had phallic symbols in them. To us the temples were interesting but hardly places in which to worship God.

It was rumored that Kali had come to Ludhiana. Tales of her miracles were widespread: people slashed their tongues with razor blades and were instantly and completely healed, or so it was rumored.

Some ten days after the first reports, we came face to face with her reality.

As her staunch devotee, Ram Lal put his faith to the test. Late one night, with a razor-sharp knife, he slashed his throat from ear to ear, not once, but seven times. To his astonishment, Kali did not heal him instantly.

Hemorrhaging furiously, his friends took him to the local government hospital. The doctor on duty took one look at him and sent him to us.

His wounds were obvious, for he had severed his windpipe just above the larynx. This lay exposed, his vocal cords moving as he breathed and vainly tried to talk. Just to breathe, he was forced to keep his head back to keep his larynx exposed. Through good luck, he had not cut any major arteries. In the operating room it took us four hours to piece him back together.

To our mutual delight, he made a prompt and complete recovery and in ten days was ready for discharge. The hospital evangelist saw this as an opportunity to make a convert. He spent many long hours with Ram Lal, explaining to him how the Christian doctors had saved his life when Kali failed him. Surely, Ram Lal would want to become a Christian.

However, Ram Lal was true to his beliefs, "I was saved by Kali."

Not to be outdone, the evangelist answered "It was Dr. Eggleston and his team who saved you."

Ram Lal was not to be put off: "Don't you understand? Dr. Eggleston is only Kali's agent."

Although the caste system was legally outlawed, it continued to flourish. Tragically, it even tainted the Christian community. Many Christians in North India came from families that had been outcastes or members of the lower castes of Hindu society. Some felt stigmatized and ashamed of their heritage.

We never realized the depth of this until Sheela stopped me on the street as I was walking home. She said she wanted to say goodbye; she was leaving Ludhiana the next day.

Sheela Masih was an excellent operating room nurse, one with whom I had worked for a long time. I asked her if she were joking or really leaving.

"Yes," she answered, "I am going to Rupar tomorrow."

Rupar was a small dusty city about ninety miles to the east at the foothills of the Himalayan mountains.

"Why are you going—is it for a better salary, or are you getting married?"

"No, I just have to leave."

"Why? You have a good job here, and your family is here in Ludhiana."

"That's the problem, my family is here."

"Are they trying to arrange a marriage for you?"

"No. My problem is that my parents are sweepers, and everyone knows it. If I stay in Ludhiana, I will always be known as a sweeper's daughter. If I go away, no one will know my background."

Yet this was not always the case, for we met many Christians, including some high in the church hierarchy, who spoke openly with pride of their humble beginnings.

*Sadhus** had an amazing grip on their followers.

Bhaktori lived in a one-room hovel across the street from us. He and his wife were sweepers, earning just enough to feed themselves and their two children, a daughter and a dim-witted son. Being staunch Hindus, they observed all feasts and celebrations with gusto.

Shortly after Christmas, their daughter Santosh, a dull girl, became sick and died after a protracted illness.

The following summer a sadhu visited Bhaktori, dragging a young buffalo calf behind him. The next day I saw the calf tethered in front of Bhaktori's house. We were concerned, for Bhaktori could ill afford this unnecessary burden.

When next I met him, I asked, "Bhaktori, do you have a new buffalo?"

---

*Sadhus are Hindu holy men who wander the streets and live off alms from the faithful.

"I bought him last week, sahib."

"Why? It is a male, and cannot give milk, and you have no place to pasture it."

"I had to."

I said that I did not understand.

Bhaktori went on, "The sadhu told me I had to."

"You do not have to do everything the sadhu tells you."

"Doctor, you do not understand. The sadhu told me that this calf is the reincarnation of our daughter. How could I not take her back?"

CHAPTER 21

Yusuf

WE HAD A COOK.

Before we arrived in India, Dr. Snow had sent Yusuf Colvin from Ludhiana to Jubar to work for us. Yusuf was reputed to speak good English, something we could never confirm.

The idea of having or even wanting a cook or any servant had never occurred to us. As we were to learn, we needed one since Barbara was soon working full time, as well as teaching our children.

Housekeeping changed. Frozen and prepared foods became but a memory. Milk arrived in a pail of questionable cleanliness and had to be boiled, as did our water. Chickens came from the market alive and squawking. In addition, in the nearby shops no one spoke English and Barbara had not yet learned Hindustani,* the local language.

However, there were compensations. We sampled new fruits and vegetables. Some fruits such as mangoes of many types, colors and sizes, guavas, papayas, fresh coconuts, and litchis with their crinkly brown skin soon became favorites. Others, such as gooseberries (ground cherries) made tart jams, and patwa (roselle) substituted for cranberry sauce. The new vegetables did not appeal as much—lauki (a gourd) seemed bland and tasteless, and karela (also a gourd) was bitter.

---

*A combination of Urdu and Hindi, using Hindi script, Hindustani is widely spoken in northwest India.

Where Is God Not?

Yusuf Colvin soon made himself one of the family. Had we had to choose a cook ourselves, we could not have done better. He worked for us for the next thirty-two years until he died, the victim of a hit-and-run driver.

Yusuf, or Joseph, as he sometimes called himself, was of uncertain age, probably a year or two older than me. Raised in a Methodist community in Pauri Garhwal, a remote area of the mountains, his education had been minimal, probably up to the fifth grade. Although able to write enough to keep his accounts, he used his fingers to help in addition. His cooking was excellent, making up for any deficiencies.

Yusuf was alone when we first met him, his family still in Pauri Garhwal. Five weeks later he got a letter from his wife telling him that one of his children had died six weeks earlier, and that a daughter had been born a week later. To add to his woes, his only cow had fallen down the hillside and been killed. He asked us for a loan and permission to bring them to Jubar. Since there were quarters for servants, and Garhwal was having one of its periodic famines, we agreed, and a few days later his wife, three sons, and an infant daughter arrived and were settled in a two-room house near us.

The youngest boy, Masih Charan, was four years old, but still unable to walk. His protuberant belly suggested that he had kwashiorkor, the result of chronic malnutrition. We wondered what Yusuf and his family thought when they saw our two well-nourished children. Powered milk and other nutritional supplements, many from the occasional CARE packages the hospital received, were available, and soon we were rewarded by seeing Masih Charan walk and the other children gain weight and strength.

Yusuf was an innovator. One evening he asked for a food grater. When Barbara said she did not have one, he took a piece of tin and hammered a nail through it in many places, letting the metal protrude on the opposite side. Turning it over, he had his grater. For years it served satisfactorily.

Yusuf was simple and completely honest in our home, something for which we were thankful. If we left money or valuables around, he scolded us, and warned us that other Indians were not as honest.

However, when it came to shopping for our food, it was a different matter. When Carol was ten, he took her with him to the local market. Bargaining furiously, he purchased the necessary vegetables and fruits, and returned home. That evening when Barbara was doing the *hissab* or household accounts with him, Carol happened to be present. When Yusuf said that the carrots cost one rupee and fifty paisa, Carol piped up, "No, Yusuf, you paid only one rupee and twenty-five paisa. Don't you remember?"

Several other items were found similarly overcharged before the accounting finally came to a merciful end. That was the last time that Yusuf took Carol with him to the market.

We had always been aware that we were slightly overcharged. We had expected it. Doubtless Yusuf considered this his *huk* or right. We had a similar experience when we were in China.

Yusuf's daughter had not been baptized before coming to Jubar, so he arranged to have Padre Das, the local minister, perform the ceremony when the latter made his monthly visit. All went smoothly until Padre Das asked what the girl's name was.

"Laxmi," said Yusuf.

Laxmi was the name of the Hindu goddess of wealth.

"But Laxmi is not a name from the Bible," Padre replied. "You must have a Christian name."

Yusuf and his wife consulted briefly at the back of our chapel.

"We will name her Rosaline."

So the infant became Rosaline. How he chose that name and why Padre Das accepted it, we never learned. Yusuf was so happy with this name that he had his second daughter baptized Sarosaline.

Like most Indian fathers, Yusuf wanted to arrange good marriages for his children. When his oldest son, Francis, reached the appropriate age, Yusuf started the search for a suitable bride. He wrote his relatives and informed his friends of his son's availability, and sat back to await results. We were not concerned about Francis's prospects, for he seemed a decent and hardworking young man with a respectable job. He was a good catch.

Soon Yusuf requested a few days off to go to Amritsar, eighty-five miles to the west to look over a prospect. When we asked about the girl he showed us her picture. To our eyes, she seemed very attractive.

Accompanied by a relative, Yusuf, set off. Francis did not go along, for the decision was not his.

Yusuf returned crestfallen, the girl was not acceptable.

"Why?" we asked.

"She is very nice, but her father is a leper."

Although the girl had been born to parents with leprosy, she had been taken from her family when she was an infant and raised in a Christian home for "untainted" children of lepers. We knew that there was no danger of leprosy to the girl, Francis, or his family. But prejudice dies hard, and Yusuf refused to reconsider.

A couple of months later Yusuf and his older brother, also in need of a bride for his son, went to Bareilly, a city nine hours by train to the east. They had learned of two Christian sisters who were looking for husbands. Before they left, they reached an agreement on which girl would be considered for Francis, and which for the brother's son. Again Francis stayed home.

Two days later a dejected Yusuf returned. Both girls were available, but his brother had changed his mind, and selected for his own son the girl originally proposed for Francis. Being older, his brother's decision was final. The other girl did not measure up to Yusuf's standards. As before, we had seen her picture, and thought her really beautiful. Yusuf had decided she would not do—she was "too dark."

So the search continued. A third candidate soon entered the contest. This time it was a school teacher from a mountain village in Pauri Garhwal near Yusuf's home. So to the mountains went Yusuf.

This time success. The girl met Yusuf's approval and the families agreed on a "bride price" of five hundred rupees. Yusuf paid gratefully and returned to Ludhiana a happy man. He, Francis, and the rest of the family would return to Pauri in a few weeks to finalize the arrangements.

The whole family went with him on the second visit. However, in the meantime, the girl's father thought that he could make a better bargain and raised the price of the prospective bride to a thousand rupees. Yusuf was rightly incensed, and ready to leave when Francis whispered in his ear, "Papa, I like her." So Yusuf paid. A date was set for the marriage and they returned to Ludhiana.

A few weeks later the wedding party set off, the marriage to take place the day after they reached the village.

The party returned, crestfallen. When they arrived at the girl's home, they found that no arrangements had been made, and the girl was off in a distant village teaching school.

Yusuf and his party were understandably outraged and demanded that the arrangements be remade. They would return in two weeks for the wedding.

This they did, and finally Francis was married.

Several times Yusuf made it clear that he intended to get the maximum price for his daughters. The thought of marriage without a substantial "bride price" was unacceptable. He had paid a heavy price for his oldest son's wife and hoped to recoup some of the cost. Besides which, he still had another four sons to be married off and only two daughters.

A year after Francis's marriage, Rosaline ran away with an electrician's helper, eliminating any hope of financial benefit for Yusuf. As if that were not enough, Rosaline's choice was also "too dark." Rosaline and her boyfriend were banished from the family in disgrace.

Three months later the couple returned to Ludhiana wanting to get married. Rev. Stevens, the minister at Kalvari Church, faced with a fait accompli, performed the ceremony quietly, without Yusuf's knowledge. He knew that Yusuf would never approve and might disrupt the proceedings.

Yusuf was a kind man at heart, and when Rosaline's first child, a boy, was born, all was forgiven and he welcomed her back.

Although Yusuf forgave his daughter, he did not forgive the padre, and left Kalvari Church. Not wanting to be without a church, when approached by a local Pentecostal communion, he, his wife, and the rest of the family joined it.

The Pentecostals would not recognize Yusuf's family's previous baptism, and insisted that he and his family be baptized again. They were taken to the Budda Nulla, a small and heavily polluted stream nearby and baptized, this time by immersion. He was now happy.

The Pentecostals had no church building, and held their services in the homes of their followers. This suited Yusuf well enough, until his turn came.

He asked Barbara if he could borrow some plastic glasses as he was expected to serve tea after the service. Barbara agreed, and lent him ours. Before the service he returned them, and asked to exchange them for smaller glasses, so that he could save money.

His relationship with the Pentecostals ended a year later when he again served as host. At their services everybody left their footwear outside when they entered the room chosen for worship. When the service was over, he found that someone had stolen his new sandals and substituted a broken pair in their place.

The following Sunday Yusuf and his family rejoined Kalvari Church.

On our return from our first furlough in 1960, we were assigned a different house. Our new home was next to the church and on the main road. We found that we had inherited a *mali*, or gardener. Ishar Das had been working for the previous occupants and, as was local custom, anticipated being given a job by their successors. We had not foreseen this, but living next to the main road we were vulnerable to sneak thieves and the appeals of the many beggars passing by. Mali Ishar Das, besides taking care of the garden, served as watchman. He was to serve us faithfully for over a quarter century.

In theory the garden was ours; in fact it was Mali who ultimately determined what grew and what did not. The flowers and vegetables that met his approval flourished, those that did not, rarely survived. We learned not to reason why.

Like most of the malis working at the hospital, he came from Pratapgarh, a town four hundred miles to the east and south of Ludhiana, a center of conservative Hinduism. Because he was orthodox in his faith, our hunting of *nilghai* raised problems for him.

Nilghai, meaning blue cow or blue bull, were large animals of the antelope family. Their meat was tasty and a welcome relief from the monotony of tough stringy goat. During the early 1960s they roamed the countryside at will. Having large appetites, they were a scourge to the farmers, for they went through wheat fields like reapers. They were so destructive that farmers came to our house, pleading with us to hunt them and protect their crops. This we did for five years, until the number of animals was under control. When the animals became scarce, we stopped hunting completely.

We did our own butchering at night outside the kitchen. When Mali would report for work the next morning, he took great pains not to come near our work area, choosing to go completely around the house rather than pass within ten feet of any bloodstain. When Barbara suggested that the blood would make an excellent fertilizer for the roses, he made it clear that she had to chose between his beliefs and her roses.

One of Mali's jobs was to fill the water tank on the roof. This he did faithfully, manning an old hand pump each morning. One day, in the middle of my shower, the tank went dry. With soap in my eyes, I sought Mali out to scold him. He was adamant, he would pump water no more. When asked why, he pointed to the pipe leading from the pump to the tank. There fixed to the wall next to the pipe were the horns of the nilghai we had shot the evening before. Our Bobby had found a place to mount them. After much discussion, Mali did agree to pump water for us, but only after I took the horns down.

Up to that time, Mali had cooked his food in our backyard, using water from our tank. Never again, for he made it clear that the water had now been defiled, and did not cook his rice properly.

Besides his aversion to blood and horns, other parts of the body were not to be touched.

One hot summer day he came to Barbara asking for a string. Our dog, Brownie, had left a bone in the middle of our backyard, and Mali refused to touch it. He wanted to loop the string around the bone and drag it away. Otherwise, it would stay there and he would not cut the grass.

He also had a great reverence for life. On the dirt path to our house there was a colony of ants. They flourished, helped by a daily ration of rice or crumbs. Ishar Das did not want them to go hungry. Nor did he ever kill any of the snakes that he occasionally uncovered in the garden, preferring to relocate them further from the house. Barbara would rather have seen them dead, particularly after her experience with a krait.

After returning from Jubar late one Sunday night, in the middle of a monsoon deluge, I was called to the hospital for an emergency. I left Barbara sitting on the bed, debating whether to go to sleep or to unpack our bags. As she looked down, a snake slithered by, an inch from her foot, closely followed by Brownie. Barbara shouted for Brownie to get out of the room, and, for one of the rare times in her life, she obeyed. The snake sought refuge under a desk in the corner. Barbara armed herself with a cane, but was afraid to attack the snake that was by now out of reach. As they eyed each other warily, the lights went out. Since I had taken our only flashlight, she had only the light from the candle we kept by our bed. After what seemed an eternity, the lights came back on. When I returned a few minutes later, she was more glad to see me than any time since our marriage. I dispatched the snake just as it was disappearing under the closet door.

The next day we identified our unwelcome visitor as a twenty-six-inch-long krait, the deadliest snake in India. Barbara then had every chink and cranny through which a snake could enter the house sealed.

In addition to snakes being sacred, so were pepul trees, peacocks, elephants, cattle, and, to some of the more orthodox, rats. On a trip to south India, we had occasion to visit a temple dedicated to the latter, where the temple grounds were honey-combed with thousands of holes leading to their nests.

In New Delhi, we once saw an elderly gentleman walk to an island between two streams of heavy traffic. In his hand was a rat trap. This he opened letting a huge rat inside escape, only to be run over. Now he could soothe his conscience, for he had not killed the rat himself.

Jain** priests carried the concept of sanctity of life to the extreme. They wore masks so as not to inhale any living insect and swept the path in front of them to avoid stepping on ants. When one of our Jain friends invited us to dinner, he stressed that we would have to eat before sundown so that moths and other insects would not be attracted to lights at the table.

Jains were vegetarians and rarely engaged in farming for fear of killing worms and the like when plowing. Having thus been forced into business, they soon became a rich community.

**An offshoot of Hinduism, Jainism developed under the leadership of the sixth-century ascetic, Mahavira.

Balbir

BALBIR'S HOPES OF BECOMING A MOTOR MECHANIC WERE fading.

Sadhu Ram and his wife, Bachni, appeared on our doorstep late one evening. They had just received word that Balbir, their oldest son, could not take his final examination to become a certified motor mechanic.

We knew the family well. Sadhu and Bachni had worked for many years as sweepers in Jubar before the sanatorium closed. They had then come to Ludhiana where we had helped them to get jobs at the medical college. Sadhu had never been to school and his wife could barely write her name.

A year earlier they had come to us for advice about Balbir's future, wanting a better life for him. Since Balbir had shown an interest in becoming a motor mechanic and there was a great shortage of them, we had encouraged him and promised to help.

Barbara arranged to get him admitted to the Christian vocational training institute at Suranussi, thirty-five miles away. In the application, she had clearly written that Balbir had passed the seventh class (grade) but failed the eighth, and therefore, in the local parlance, was "eighth-class failed."

Supported by our recommendation (and financial help), Balbir was admitted and started his course. Periodically we received word that he was doing well in his studies, so all were happy. After completing ten months, Balbir had been asked to produce his "eighth-class pass" certificate—something he obviously did not have. The government required all students to produce it at the time of the examinations.

We were upset, for we felt personally responsible.

Suddenly, Sadhu had an idea. He could get a certificate on the black market for 500 rupees, the equivalent of three weeks salary. What did we think of that? And would we pay for it?

Needless to say, we did not think much of this idea, although we were aware that it was an everyday practice. We also knew that the village school near Jubar where Balbir had studied was one of many throughout the land with few if any books, one which provided little real education. Every year many students failed.

Since Balbir had done well in his training, we were sympathetic to his cause and realized that he would probably never have another chance to better himself.

We discussed this problem with many of our friends. They were divided on what we should advise Sadhu and Bachni. One conservative missionary said that of course Balbir should repeat the eighth class and then his motor mechanic course. We pointed out that he would then lose two full years, through no fault of his own. No matter, the missionary said, we should teach him a lesson. We never quite understood what lesson he meant.

Others said that since the fault was not his, he should not suffer. But what about a dishonest certificate, we asked?

The reply was "as it is common, why worry?"

Fortunately for our consciences, before we had time to advise him, Balbir appeared at our door with his government certificate. We knew the answer.

Balbir passed his examination and became a motor mechanic.

What was right?

CHAPTER 23

You Are Not Alone

"DR. EGGLESTON, WILL YOU BE THE NEXT DIRECTOR?"

It was mid-July and I was making rounds on the female surgical ward when Dr. Nambudripad, the head of the institution, called me to his office. Sitting with him were Father Kenneth Sharp, an Anglican priest who was the chairman of the governing body, and Dr. Jai Khristmukti, the vice-chairman, both old friends.

Father Sharp went on "Dr. Nambudripad has served as director for eight years and thinks it is time to step down."

The institution had been stagnating. Morale was poor, the result of a combination of low salaries and failure to encourage clinical and research work.

In the spring of 1982 over eighty of the staff sent a petition to the governing body with a long list of grievances. The latter had responded by appointing a committee to study the problem. In their report they urged a change in administration.

Father Sharp went on, "Dr. Nambudripad thinks that you should be the next director. So do I."

"I don't agree. The next director should be an Indian. I feel strongly about this."

Dr. Nambudripad joined in, "While I would like to agree with you, you have served the institution for twenty-nine years and know it and understand its problems as well as anyone."

Again I recommended that they appoint an Indian, not a foreigner.

All three of them asked me to reconsider. I agreed to, but only after consulting with Barbara.

The Department of Surgery was in the process of developing new specialities, including an open-heart program. Treating patients and teaching medical students appealed to me much more than administration. In addition, we were involved in a couple of small but interesting research projects. Most of all, I enjoyed guiding our surgical residents in their training on the wards and in the operating room. Seeing them progress was my greatest pleasure. Were I to agree, I would have to curtail or even abandon these interests.

Unfortunately, there was a shortage of Christian staff with administrative experience, and at least I had run a hospital (Jubar) for twenty years. Earlier I had also served as medical superintendent of the hospital for eighteen months.

Several days later Dr. Nambudripad showed me a letter that Father Sharp had written after returning to his home in Delhi. Several members of the governing body, as well as some of the staff, had asked him to convince me to take the job.

All this appealed to my vanity. The opportunity to encourage our staff to develop new areas of work, to stimulate research, and to improve the institution was challenging. On the other hand, when I thought of the many petty jealousies dividing the staff, personality clashes, severe financial constraints, and dozens of other problems, the job seemed less desirable.

The monthly institutional communion service in August seemed directed at me. The hymn, "What a Friend We Have in Jesus," reminded me that He would always be there. Then in Rev. Jaiwant Noel's sermon, the words "a living sacrifice" suggested to me that was what I might become. Rev. Noel also reminded us that is what Christians are called to be.

Many members of the staff came to me, urging me to accept. Others no doubt felt the other way. I still could not decide. Rev. Noel, a close friend and ever a constant support, urged me to accept.

With Barabara at the time I was appointed director in 1982.

Naturally, I turned to my closest and most faithful adviser, Barbara. As was usual, she was more than candid, "You know that you will accept, and that you will never forgive yourself if you do not."

Finally, after much thought and prayer, I did agree to allow my name to be considered at the next governing body meeting. On August 17, 1982, the governing body unanimously elected me director, to take charge on the nineteenth.

We knew that the Presbyterian Church rightly discouraged missionaries from heading institutions overseas. When they learned the reasons for my appointment, they not only accepted the decision, but backed us completely.

Father Sharp and Rev. Noel were anxious to have an installation service. This I opposed, for no such ceremony had been held in the past twenty-nine years. They made it clear that the choice was not mine.

During the month before my appointment, I had spent many sleepless hours reflecting on my inadequacies for the job and the problems confronting the institution. The installation service provided me the answer for which I had been searching, the answer that should have been obvious. During a prayer on my behalf, I was reminded, "You are not alone, He will guide you."

I had foolishly thought to rely only on myself.

That night as I lay in bed thinking about the future, it suddenly dawned upon me that what I would do would affect the lives of all of the seventeen hundred staff, and their families as well as the local tradesmen who depended on the institution for their livelihood. I felt inadequate, until I remembered that I would not be alone.

I never was.

CHAPTER 24

Unrest in the Punjab

THE BEST WAY WAS TO BEGIN WITH PRAYER.

The first Monday after I became director, I invited all the administrators to meet in my office after morning chapel. This was the start of what would become a weekly prayer meeting. It was there that we could bring our collective problems to God and get the strength needed for our work. It was the most important thing I did as director.

The first person to take note of my promotion was Yusuf. He promptly announced that as the director's cook, he should be paid more. Unfortunately for him, Barbara did not agree, but did compensate him when extra work became necessary.

Although we had anticipated that my appointment as director would alter our lives, the change in our relationships with our colleagues and friends came as a shock.

We had not appreciated the loneliness of administration. Our friends seemed reluctant to invite us to their homes for fear of appearing to curry favor. One professor even asked if there were a protocol to follow.

We were equally unhappy about our own response to this. Two weeks after my appointment, a member of the senior faculty and a good friend invited us to dinner. Our first, and shameful, reaction was to wonder if there were a purpose behind the invitation. Since we could hardly ask, we considered the matter at length, and finally accepted. We were pleasantly surprised when it turned out to be a birthday party for our host.

Two months later another friend remarked that Dr. Nambudripad looked ten years younger since he had returned to clinical practice and that I looked ten years older.

It was my hope that there would be peace in the Punjab. However, I was not optimistic, for trouble had been brewing in the state for many years, and was likely to escalate. There were too many hotheads in positions of power, and the government seemed unable to deal with them.

Nevertheless, by God's Grace we accomplished most of what we planned despite nearly constant civil unrest.

Punjab was a small state, approximately half the size of Ohio. Before partition in August 1947, it had been much larger, and had included land now in Pakistan. Partition had been violent, leaving an estimated half million or more dead. Muslims fled westward as Hindus and Sikhs* sought refuge to the east. In a short time the latter two became assimilated into their new surroundings, Hindus flocking to the cities to work as shopkeepers or in industry, Sikhs continuing their traditional roles as farmers or joining the military. Soon the Punjab recovered and prospered, and in time became the richest state in India, producing half of its grain. The government improved the already extensive irrigation system, extending existing canals, building new ones, and digging wells. Soon five of every six farms were irrigated. Although two-thirds of the farmers had less than five acres of land, tractors replaced bullocks, transistor radios became the norm, and television antennas sprouted from rooftops.

Hindus and Sikhs had lived in harmony for centuries, now and then intermarrying. On occasion when a Hindu woman could not produce a son, she would pray at a *gurudwara* (Sikh temple). If a son were forthcoming, he would be raised as a Sikh. Younger brothers would remain Hindu.

---

*Guru Nanak was the founder of the Sikh faith in the fifteenth century. "Sikh" means disciple. Sikhism developed by a succession of ten gurus or teachers, the first being Guru Nanak who rejected the casteism of Hinduism and accepted the brotherhood of Islam. It is a monotheistic religion.

Where Is God Not?

Nevertheless, from the time of partition, Sikh leaders had been pressing for their own state, claiming it had been promised them by the British. In 1961 Master Tara Singh, a former school teacher turned political leader, himself a convert from Hinduism during his school years, became the leader of the Akali Dal, the Sikh political party. He demanded Punjabi Suba, or a state in which Punjabi would be the official language. The central (federal) government did not agree, and Tara Singh went on a hunger strike. The government, under Prime Minister Nehru, considered this a communal problem, not a political one and held firm. Not wanting to die, Tara Singh finally gave up after a fast of forty-seven days.

Five years later, Sant Fateh Singh, another Sikh political leader, again challenged the government, now under Indira Gandhi, Nehru's daughter. Fateh Singh announced that he would fast for two weeks and immolate himself by burning unless a Punjabi-speaking state were formed. A suitable funeral pyre, visible to all, was prepared at the Golden Temple in Amritsar.

Mrs. Gandhi capitulated, and once more the Punjab was divided, this time more or less along linguistic lines. This had an amusing side. Soon all road signs were repainted in *Gurmukhi*, the written script of Punjabi. When it was realized that many people could not read them, alternate signs were repainted in their original Hindi.

As a Christian institution, we had not been much affected by the turmoil, other than caring for the occasional casualty.

In the late 1970s one casualty was Kartar Singh Bhindranwale. He was the leader of the Damdami Taksal, an influential school, dedicated to maintaining the purity of the Sikh faith. It had been founded by Baba Deep Singh, one of the heroes of the Sikhs. As such, it was important politically, for in the Punjab, as in the rest of India, religion and politics were rarely divorced from each other. Among the rules laid down by Guru Gobind Singh, the last of the ten gurus who founded Sikhism, was that Sikhs not cut any of their hair.

Kartar Singh was in a serious automobile accident near Ludhiana and admitted to our hospital. Anticipating the possibility of an operation, a surgical resident told an orderly to shave

Kartar Singh's abdomen. Immediately one of Kartar Singh's young disciples crept up besides the resident and quietly whispered in his ear, "Touch one hair and I will kill you."

Kartar Singh's hair remained intact.

Kartar Singh was admitted to our intensive care unit in an unconscious state. Soon we had to place him on a respirator. A fellow priest and close associate of his approached us and said that Kartar Singh was required to say certain prayers every day. Since he could hardly do that himself, would we allow a fellow priest to stand beside his bed and recite them for him?

We explained that we did not allow relatives or friends into the ICU outside of visiting hours, and then only for a few minutes at a time. The prayers might take a long time. The priest answered that two disciples could say the prayers for him, one would take two hours, the other a much shorter time. They would ask the latter if we agreed. This we did, and every day after that prayers were read quietly at his bedside.

Kartar Singh was badly injured, and died after a long but losing fight for his life. The future of the Punjab changed permanently when Jarnail Singh Bhindranwale succeeded him.

Tension in the Punjab continued to mount. In September of 1983 the chief of police in Ludhiana, Mr. Bhatti, was shot in broad daylight as he was entering his office accompanied by his bodyguards. The would-be assassins escaped on a motorcycle, and Mr. Bhatti was brought to our hospital. Soon swarms of policemen were everywhere, checking all patients, doctors, and other staff near his room. The bullets had shattered his arm bone but had missed the nerves and blood vessels. He recovered uneventfully.

A month later Sikh terrorists ambushed a bus on a rural road nearby and shot to death all Hindu passengers.

As 1983 drew to a close, it was rumored that Jarnail Singh Bhindranwale had ordered the Golden Temple fortified under the direction of disgruntled former army officers. The temple now served as a base from which the extremists operated.

This temple, one of the most sacred shrines of the Sikhs, was a glory of white marble, built in the center of an artificial lake. We had visited it often and admired the intricate marble inlay and paintings. It was a priceless work of art as well as a religious shrine. Many of our Sikh friends told us privately that they felt that the temple was being desecrated.

Tensions between the Hindus and Sikhs increased daily. Ears of cows were thrown into Hindu temples, a blasphemy to the Hindus. In return, cigarettes, forbidden to orthodox Sikhs, were discovered in gurudwaras.

We could only pray that 1984 would bring an improvement.

CHAPTER 25

Operation Blue Star

UNFORTUNATELY, 1984 BROUGHT NO PEACE TO THE PUNJAB.

In February the newspapers reported that Sikh extremists had killed at least seventy-seven people. March saw fanatics riding motorcycles or scooters through the bazaars, firing automatic rifles indiscriminately into stores. The government imposed a total curfew for three days and banned more than one person riding a scooter or a motorcycle.

In May the father of one of our surgical residents, a Hindu, received a letter telling him that his son was going to be killed because the latter had treated two of the terrorists' victims. The letter credited the resident with saving their lives. It ended by saying that they had given a warning because they thought (incorrectly) that the doctor's wife was a Sikh.

Since the father held a high position in the Congress party, the political party then in power, we thought that the letter might be intended to scare the father, rather than actually threaten the son. In any case, the police advised the doctor to leave the country immediately. I concurred, and he went to the Middle East the next day.

This threat alarmed us. We reasoned that if it were due to the father's political position, it posed no problem for the hospital workers. On the other hand if it were the result of our providing medical care to the victims of terrorism, then our staff could be in danger. We were not certain what to do, for the local government hospital was not equipped to handle major casualties. The district commissioner promised to provide us protection should it become necessary.

I, too, received a threatening letter. It ordered me to change the name of the Christian Medical College to the Guru Nanak Medical College immediately or my life would be forfeit. The letterhead was from Chowk Mehta, the headquarters of the terrorists near Amritsar. However, it had been postmarked in Ludhiana, far from Chowk Mehta. We sent it on to the local police for advice.

Two weeks later a policeman came to discuss the matter. Since it was written in Hindi and the terrorists were agitating for Punjabi as the official language, it was probably nothing more than a crank letter. It was not one that I enjoyed.

Early in June, the extremists announced that they would not let food grown in the Punjab leave the state. They added that they planned to disrupt the electrical power lines and divert the water in the canals passing through it. Since much of the electricity and water to the neighboring states of Haryana and Rajastan as well as New Delhi came from the mountains and traversed the Punjab, these actions would seriously hurt millions. The government responded by sending in the army to restore law and order. At night military vehicles rumbled through the streets as troops moved toward Amritsar.

A curfew and news blackout soon followed. Fortunately, in anticipation of further unrest and possible violence, I had ordered our maintenance staff to purchase as much diesel and gasoline as they could store. We were to need them.

A few days later, on Sunday, June 3, it was announced on the radio that all foreigners in the Punjab were to register with the police immediately. Mr. Vijay Ooman, our capable personnel officer, took a list of all of them to the police.

That night a total curfew was imposed.

Several members of our staff were arrested trying to come to work the next morning. Fortunately, we were able to get them released, but only with great difficulty. The police warned them to stay at home.

We reviewed the situation and found that we were out of oxygen, short of surgical gloves, and in need of food for our patients, students, and staff. Hoping that the military would allow our ambulance to pass, I drove across the city with Mr. Ooman and Dr. Richard Daniel, the medical superintendent, to discuss the situation with the assistant district commissioner (ADC). The streets, ever teeming with people and traffic, were totally deserted save for the police and heavily armed army units. Store fronts were shuttered, and all business at a standstill.

The ADC proved very helpful. We explained that we had a community of over fifteen hundred dependent upon us. We needed oxygen for the patients and food for all, especially milk for the babies in the nursery and on the pediatric wards. The ADC issued the necessary orders, and gave us a pass for one ambulance. He also arranged for the local oxygen factory to fill our cylinders.

Being cut off from all outside telephone facilities, telegraph service, newspapers, and mail, we relied on our radio for information about what was going on. We listened to the news stations—All India Radio (AIR), the Voice of America (VOA), Radio Australia, and the British Broadcasting Corporation (BBC). The latter two proved the most reliable, for All India Radio's news was heavily censored, and the VOA gave little heed to India.

Wednesday, the third day of total curfew, the district commissioner's office telephoned me late at night ordering us to have the hospital ready to receive heavy casualties. That evening the army entered the Golden Temple and other Sikh temples throughout the state. Fortunately, no casualties occurred in our area.

The assault on the Golden Temple tragically coincided with the day Guru Arjun Dev's martyrdom was celebrated. Arjun Dev, the fifth of the ten Sikh gurus, had been the builder of the Golden Temple. As a result, there were nearly a thousand pilgrims within the Temple complex.

Where Is God Not?

Operation Blue Star, as it was code named, was nothing short of a full-fledged military operation, complete with tanks. How many died will never be known, but it numbered in the many hundreds.

The next morning All India Radio announced that the army had entered the Golden Temple and that Bhindranwale along with other leaders of the extremists had been killed. Immediately scores of inflamed Sikhs poured onto the nearby rooftops shouting and screaming all manner of imprecations. There were riots in Delhi and nearby cities. In protest, Sikh military personnel throughout the country returned their hard-earned military decorations and honors to the government. Sikh politicians in the Congress party resigned to join other parties.

Despite the continuing curfew in Ludhiana, Sikh priests from the gurudwara across the street from the hospital obtained permission to hold a *langer** in our parking lot. This helped us greatly as they fed the relatives of our patients for whom we were unable to provide. We thanked them gratefully.

Ultimately, after five and a half days, the curfew was relaxed for three hours to allow people to buy food. When a few shop-keepers attempted to profiteer by raising prices outrageously, the military confiscated the food and gave it to delighted house-wives. Milk they gave to our hospital.

Over the next few days the situation remained tense amid unfounded rumors of Bhindranwale's survival. Some Sikh soldiers mutinied against their superiors. Little was done to allay the tension, and communal feelings rose. Our inpatient census dropped nearly in half and outpatients (normally about eight hundred daily) stopped coming. Our income went down ten thousand dollars a day. As a result we were forced to postpone plans to build much-needed apartments for our faculty.

As always, the most affected were the poor, particularly the thousands of "daily wage" workers, few of whom had any savings. Many simply went hungry.

---

*Every gurudwara of size had a dining room called a langer attached to it where food was served free to all regardless of caste, creed, and race. The only conditions were that everybody eat the same food and sit together.

Conditions in the Punjab improved gradually over the next few weeks. The military remained in charge, patrolling the streets and imposing restrictions on travel, particularly at night. For months no trains or buses ran after sunset for fear of sabotage or ambush. Gradually patients returned, and our finances slowly improved.

Within our institution we had our own share of problems.

One Sunday evening while at church, I received an urgent message to go to the construction site of our new medical college building. There had been an accident while excavating the foundations. It had rained hard the previous day, and the contractor had stopped work. On Sunday, although the dirt was still very soft, he resumed digging. The south wall of the site had collapsed, burying one of the workers.

At the bottom of the pit a body lay motionless. The foreman told me that Ram Jee Das was dead. I descended some fifteen or twenty feet down a rickety bamboo ladder, fervently praying that there would be no more cave-ins. Ram Jee Das was certainly dead, his skull crushed and his face distorted almost beyond recognition. He never knew what happened. The contractors had fled, rightly fearing the wrath of the rest of the workers, most of whom came from the victim's village.

Ram Jee Das's relatives wanted to take the body away. We persuaded them to take it to our hospital to make certain that there would be a written record of the accident. This was done and the matter reported to the police, from whom we (correctly) anticipated no help.

The man killed was a *bayia*, or a migrant laborer from Bihar, the most backward state in India. Bayias, among the poorest of the world's poor, left their families at home and traveled many hundreds of miles in search of work of any sort. They went by train, perched on the top of passenger cars to avoid buying tickets, some falling to their deaths on the way. The Punjab was a favorite destination, for factories needed workers, as did farmers during the harvest season. Bayias were not afraid of terrorists, for they had nothing to lose. Labor contractors and farmers met the trains and carted the men off in their trucks, bribing the train officials. If the bayias objected, then the contractors would threaten to turn them over to the railway police. The bayias led hard lives, but depended on these jobs for survival.

When we met with the contractors the next morning, they were totally unconcerned. Their only worry was whether the other workers would stay on the job. On the other hand, we were concerned for Ram Jee Das's family. There was no workman's compensation for migrant workers, and we knew that the contractors would never offer any compensation if they could avoid it. We were finally able to obtain a pittance, the equivalent of two months pay. This was given to his nephew who had been working alongside him. Whether Ram Jee Das's family ever received any of the money or not, we never knew.

The government was aware of the problem of industrial accidents and the need for protecting workers. They administered the Employees State Insurance scheme (ESI) which ran hospitals and provided medical care for factory workers. It was not a comprehensive program, and farm workers and migrant laborers were rarely covered.

Many laborers were brought to us having had fingers, hands, or even arms completely amputated by fodder choppers or other mechanized equipment. Often their employers took them to the emergency room and departed, some leaving a small (and usually inadequate) sum to pay for their care, others nothing at all. Few showed much concern; most never returned.

We doctors campaigned for safety devices on dangerous equipment. But these were often removed, particularly when they diminished the output of the worker.

Fortunately, one of our faculty, Dr. A. B. Thomas, developed an interest in microsurgery and soon could reattach these severed parts. He opened the first training program in this field of surgery in India.

The university examinations had been delayed several months due to threats by the terrorists to disrupt them.

In the middle of July the district commissioner summoned the principals of the forty-one colleges in our district (county) to his office. Along with other local officials were senior army officers. The district commissioner announced that the examinations would be rescheduled and held anyway. When several Sikh principals expressed fear for their students in the rural areas, the army guaranteed everybody protection.

The army did its job well. Our examination hall was surrounded by security staff and all students searched before entering it. The exams took place without incident.

CHAPTER 26

Assassination

"THE BITCH IS DEAD." THE STUDENTS IN ONE OF THE SIKH colleges were celebrating.

Mrs. Indira Gandhi, the prime minister, had been brutally gunned down by two of her bodyguards, both Sikhs.

Mrs. Gandhi had ignored the recommendation of her advisors to replace these two and on the last day of October 1984 they gunned her down in the courtyard of her home. Ironically, she was wearing a saffron sari, and saffron is the color of martyrdom in Sikhism. What made it more outrageous was that Mrs. Gandhi herself had been paying for the education of the children of one of her assassins.

The reaction in Ludhiana was instantaneous. In the streets there was wild jubilation, with Sikh shopkeepers celebrating by passing out sweets (candies) to bystanders.

As a mark of respect, we closed the college and hospital. We sent letters of condolence to the president of India, Giani Zial Singh and Rajiv Gandhi, Mrs. Gandhi's son, who succeeded his mother as prime minister.

The radio reported that presidents and heads of state throughout the world would attend the cremation. The United States would send their secretary of state. We were disappointed, for it was anticipated that the president of the United States, his wife or, at a minimum, the vice-president would come.

After a lengthy debate, we decided to hold a memorial service. Mrs. Gandhi had been the prime minister and a staunch protector of the minorities in the country, including the Christians. We planned to have a Christian, a Hindu, and a Sikh each say something about her and her life. We wondered if any Sikh would be willing to do this, but one of our faculty, a former army officer, said he would, for he was one of the many Sikhs who decried the violence.

However, a few hours before the service, we had second thoughts. With passions escalating in Delhi and other large cities of North India, we felt that we might expose him to needless criticism and possible retaliation. Instead, we held a simple service, with Bible readings and hymns, and no eulogies. It ended with prayers for peace, forgiveness, and reconciliation. We mourned with Rajiv Gandhi, not for the loss of a political figure, but for the loss of a mother.

The service was sparsely attended, and only one Sikh present. Such were the emotions of the time.

The assassination taught us to question the value of a completely free press. The BBC and Radio Australia carried reports that only added fuel to fires, already well-stoked. Besides providing eyewitness accounts of Sikhs being torched to death by Hindus with gasoline-filled tires around their necks, they recounted other equally gruesome acts. The BBC aired interviews with Indians in England that were highly inflammatory. Restraint would have been welcome.

Radio Moscow, as could have been predicted, claimed that there might have been foreign involvement in the assassination.

While violence was the order of the day outside the Punjab, there was less in Ludhiana, although the atmosphere in the bazaars was tense. The reason was simple—the violence was done only in areas where Hindus greatly outnumbered Sikhs. In the Punjab the two factions were nearly evenly balanced.

On the day of the assassination three members of our staff were traveling by train to Bombay to clear a shipment from the USA through customs. One of them was a Sikh, easily identifiable by his beard and turban. Hindu mobs stopped the train just outside Delhi looking for Sikhs to kill. Fortunately, our staff shared a compartment with two army men, one a Christian, the other a Hindu. They hid the Sikh under the seat, surrounding him with luggage and protected him. He was possibly the only Sikh on the train to reach Bombay alive.

A week later we were still under night curfew, the Punjab sealed off and without mail delivery. Censorship of the newspapers continued, and the army patrolled the streets. The government closed the schools and colleges for two weeks. Many of our students had to remain confined to the campus, for they lived far from Ludhiana and travel was difficult. An angry Sikh mob chased one of our interns through the streets. Fortunately he escaped unharmed.

In other states Sikhs who felt threatened by the local Hindu community shaved their beards and had their hair cut for the first time. Barbers exploited the situation, charging fees of five hundred rupees or more, a hundred times the going rate. This they justified on the basis that they were at risk for dealing with Sikhs.

One tragic aftermath was a deluge of Sikh refugees from neighboring states. Gurudwaras quartered as many as they could. For the next six months, Sikh doctors who had fled for their lives approached us for jobs. We were able to employ some.

India had suffered another disaster.

Soon new attempts were made at rapprochement between the government in Delhi and the Sikhs in the Punjab. We rejoiced when Sant Harcharan Singh Longowal, a much respected and moderate Sikh leader, met with Rajiv Gandhi and in less than forty-eight hours reached a settlement.

On his return to the Punjab, Longowal stopped at a gurudwara in Sangrur, a town sixty miles east of Ludhiana. There he was gunned down along with some of his followers.

Our hospital was notified that he and other casualties would be brought to our hospital, despite there being a good government medical college hospital at Patiala, only twenty miles from Sangrur.

The staff was alerted and rallied splendidly. However, Longowal had died on the spot. Instead, three others were brought by car. One, a very close associate of Longowal's had been shot in the abdomen. When he was wheeled into the hospital, he looked up and asked, "Where have you taken me?"

One of his friends replied, "To the Christian Medical College Hospital."

The patient answered, "Thank God. I don't have to worry."

Such was our reputation.

CHAPTER 27

No, You Would Never Do That

"DR. EGGLESTON, WILL YOU DO ME A FAVOR?"

My inward feeling was very different from my reply, "What is it?"

"My niece has applied to your institution for a residency in obstetrics and gynecology. Will you help her get one?"

I was sitting in the office of the Punjab state health secretary, a lady rightly noted for her toughness. Dr. Mary Matthew, the principal of the medical college, and I along with another of our faculty had gone to get a grant-in-aid for our institution. It had already been sanctioned, and should have been no problem, but, as was frequently the case, the authorities had delayed payment. We had been warned that we would lose it unless I pressed the matter personally.

We had travelled the nearly two-hour sixty-mile trip to the capital in Chandigarh. After a brief wait, we had been ushered into Madam Secretary's office. We had scarcely time to sit down when she launched into a long diatribe about the Christian Medical College and its hospital. For more than twenty minutes she enumerated every fault possible, both real and imaginary. She claimed that we overcharged our patients, that we had no concern for the poor, that our teaching was poor and so forth. We answered as best we could, pointing out that we treated all patients equally, regardless of their religion or background. If they had no money, they were not charged. We reminded her that this cost the hospital over 2,200,000 rupees annually ($220,000).

She went on to complain that our tuition was excessive. We pointed out that our students paid less than half the cost of their education, and that we offered generous scholarships and loans for those in need.

But there was no way to satisfy her. She continued her harangue unabated. Finally, after reminding her of the purpose of our visit, we said that we must not take more of her time and left.

No sooner had we started down the corridor, than she sent a messenger, asking me to return without the others. I wondered what new bedevilment she had now conjured up.

But now she was all charm and kindness. She wanted us to train her niece. I explained to her that I could do nothing to interfere with our selection system which was based on an examination and a commitment to work in a Christian institution. Her niece was free to apply and compete with her peers.

Despite her antagonism, and her niece not being selected, we ultimately received our grant.

Such requests for favoritism were common.

Later that year another unpleasant incident arose at the time of selection of medical students. Admission to the medical college was highly competitive with over 2,500 applications for only fifty places. We were under constant pressure by friends, relatives, and others for "special consideration." To avoid favoritism we had introduced a system whereby candidates' names and role numbers were not known to the admission committee. This "blind" system which rewarded merit had served us well over the years.

One Sunday morning a few days before the admission committee was to meet, Dr. Gopal came to my house to see me. He was an undersecretary in the Health Ministry in New Delhi. I had dealt with him on institutional matters several times in the past. He had usually been helpful.

After the usual pleasantries and cups of tea, he came directly to the point.

"Dr. Eggleston, my nephew has applied for admission to the Christian Medical College. I want him admitted."

I told him that we had a selection committee and it was in their hands. In any case, all admissions were made on merit.

He was not satisfied.

"Dr. Eggleston, let me remind you that every paper concerning this college and hospital that goes to the government crosses my desk for my comments. In addition, it was I who helped you to get a visa for one of your staff."

He was right on both counts, and I had thanked him for his help in the past. I then reminded him that we had saved the life of another of his nephews, a year earlier, a fact which he readily acknowledged.

I outlined our procedures, to no avail. Finally, as he got up to leave, he pulled a piece of paper from his pocket with his nephew's name and roll number on it and put it down on the table. He had a final word, "You are the director of this institution. As such you can do anything you want in this matter. Furthermore, I have another nephew who will be applying next year."

I discussed the matter with the principal. Both of us realized that Dr. Gopal could hurt the institution very much should he so choose. But we both agreed that we would not give in to intimidation. We prayed that the nephew would either be selected or do so badly that he could never be considered. Were he to be first on our waiting list and not admitted, Dr. Gopal would never understand why we did not "help."

We were thankful that he did poorly and was not admitted. Had he been, Dr. Gopal would have thought that we had been influenced by his visit.

After that I tried to avoid Dr. Gopal's office whenever I had to go to Delhi. Thankfully, he was soon transferred to another department.

Early in 1984 the surgeons in the department of neurosurgery prodded the administration to purchase a CT scanner.

This magnificent but expensive piece of equipment was widely used in the West, but had only just been introduced into India, and not at all in the Punjab.

When the instrument was first developed, we had decided not to purchase one immediately, but wait until second and third generation machines became available. They would be more rugged and, hopefully, less expensive. In addition, we wanted to be certain that there were adequate facilities for maintenance within the country. Now the proper time had come. Without custom duty, it would cost $600,000.

It was mid-February, and the government was likely to pass new excise regulations by the end of the month. Unless we obtained a special exemption, we might have to pay duty of over 100 percent which was out of the question.

So off to Delhi we went. With the help of Mr. Balram Jakhar, the speaker of the parliament, everything went smoothly until we went to the Health Ministry for the final papers. All we needed was the signature of an undersecretary, Dr. Gosh. The form he gave us indicated that the scanner would be used "for research only."

We told Dr. Gosh that while we expected to do research with it, the scanner's primary use was for care of patients. I could not sign the form as written. If the limiting word "only" were deleted, there would be no problem. He said not to worry about the wording, it was a mere formality.

I repeated that we did not believe it right to sign the form as written.

Dr. Gosh replied, "Every other hospital that has imported a CT scanner has done so, for only equipment intended only for research is exempt from duty."

"We cannot sign an agreement that we have no intention of keeping."

Everybody knew that the scanners in use in New Delhi and elsewhere were not bought merely for research.

"They signed, and so must you."

Again I replied that I could not in clear conscience do so, no matter what others had done.

"But then your institution will not be able to get a scanner without paying duty."

"This will make it difficult for us to improve the care of our patients."

He continued, "No, I will not give you the certificate, unless you sign."

So I stood up, and got ready to leave. Dr. Gosh said "You really will lose this opportunity?"

I said "yes" and started out the door when Dr. Gosh suddenly turned to his clerk and said, "Do as Dr. Eggleston wants. Take out the word 'only' so that he can get it and use it for his patients."

I promptly signed.

A year later, the vice-chancellor of the Panjab University, the university to which we were affiliated, informed us that we had to replace eight of our professors. They were over the university age of retirement of sixty. We replied that we could not agree to this and that our retirement age was sixty-five.

Being a private Christian institution we did not have the financial resources of the government medical colleges, and it was difficult to recruit senior professors. An older retirement age allowed us to employ a few experienced senior faculty who had retired from the government but who were eager to work for a few more years. To lose their services and experience would hurt us greatly.

Taking our principal, Dr. Mary Matthew, and one of our senior-most professors along with me I went to Chandigarh to meet the vice-chancellor who was past the retirement age himself. After, the usual tea and pleasantries, the vice-chancellor reiterated the university's insistence that we replace the professors in question. We argued in vain. We pointed out that we were a private college run for a recognized minority (Christians) and as such had specific rights under the constitution of India.

The vice-chancellor remained adamant. We emphasized the difficulty in recruiting suitably qualified faculty due to the violence in the state.

Finally the vice-chancellor indicated that the interview was over. We returned to our car discouraged. No sooner were we seated when a messenger came running. Would Dr. Eggleston please return alone to the vice-chancellor's office?

This I did with hesitation. Although I knew that the vice-chancellor was a kind and helpful gentleman as well as a brilliant scientist, I would have preferred to have a witness with me.

"Dr. Eggleston, I well understand your problems. Is there no way in which we can work this out?"

"I don't know how."

He went on, "Its too bad that you can't alter the birth dates on the staff records."

"I wish I could, but that's impossible."

The vice-chancellor said, "No, you would never do that. Let me see what I can do for you."

We kept our faculty and heard no more on the matter until a new vice-chancellor was appointed a few years later.

CHAPTER 28

You Have Ruined Me

KAMLA WAS CRYING.

Kamla, a young Hindu woman from Delhi, had been admitted to Jubar with advanced tuberculosis. Unfortunately, her disease did not respond well to medical treatment and after six months it became obvious that part of her left lung would have to be removed. We had operated on her that morning.

I asked "Is the pain too much."

"No, there's not much."

"Then what is the matter?"

Reluctantly she asked, "Why did you treat me differently?"

"What do you mean?"

"No one prayed with me before the operation."

It was our custom to pray with our patients before they were anesthetized. That day we had been assigned a new anesthetist who had not given us time to do so before starting. We explained to Kamla that we had prayed after she was asleep. She was appeased and went on to make an uneventful recovery.

Why did Kamla want us to pray to a God other than her own? We could only hope that a seed had been planted that would blossom later. We never knew, for she soon went home well and never returned.

It was difficult to measure the impact we had as Christians. While the vast majority of patients came to the hospital because of its reputation, others came because it was a Christian institution.

Our witness was both in the quality of medicine as well as in the care and concern shown.

The chaplain and his staff visited the patients in the outpatient department and on the wards, sharing the Gospel and praying with them. Through loudspeakers brief Christian messages and songs were broadcast twice a day. On Sundays, Christian services were held on all twenty-six wards. Although 95 percent of our patients were either Sikh or Hindu, they rarely objected. Their own priests seldom, if ever, visited them. As Christians we cared about them and tried to show it. Did they know it?

Nurses played a crucial role through their work.

Durga Devi, a high-caste Hindu, was admitted to the surgical service late one evening, vomiting repeatedly and in great pain. She had an intestinal obstruction and needed an emergency operation. It became necessary to do a colostomy to save her life.

After a colostomy, patients move their bowels from an opening on their abdomen, a messy and unpleasant affair, particularly during the first few days.

Sister Masih was doing the dressing when Durga Devi suddenly looked up at her and said "You are a Christian, aren't you?"

Sister Masih wondered how Durga Devi knew, for she wore no name tag or cross.

Durga Devi went on, "Since I have had this operation, my family has rejected me. They consider me unclean and do not want to be near me. Only a Christian would do this for me with the love you have shown."

While Durga Devi may have felt this way, we knew that many of our nurses of other faiths were equally kind. Durga Devi had equated compassion with Christianity.

We probably had more influence on students than on patients, for we were in close contact with them for five and a half years or more.

They applied to the medical college for a variety of reasons. The Christians came because the institution had been founded to

We were proud of our nurses.

train Christian doctors.* They were admitted under the sponsorship of their own churches and signed agreements to return and serve in mission hospitals. Those of other faiths applied because of its reputation or because they were unable to obtain admission into the less expensive government medical colleges.

Their motivation was sometimes difficult to determine, for many applied only because of parental pressure. Fortunately most of them did well and became excellent and caring physicians.

Young women came because their parents preferred having their daughters study in a college that offered a more sheltered environment. Some parents regretted this later, for numerous unplanned romances developed. Parents traditionally expected to be the ones to select their children's spouses.

---

*When writing their constitution in 1949, India's founders recognized the need to protect the rights of the country's many minorities. Accordingly, it was expected that we would give preference to Christian candidates. This constitutional protection of minority rights was not limited to the Christian community; it extended to all minorities.

Most of the Christian staff never considered proselytizing openly, but tried to witness by example or in quiet talks. When we first arrived at Ludhiana, all students were assigned to "Friday Groups" which met weekly in the homes of the Christian staff, mostly missionaries. These groups varied greatly, some limiting their meetings to Bible study, others being more social in nature. Over the years as the number of missionaries decreased the groups also declined and gradually disappeared. But they had influenced many students, and because of them some were later baptized.

On our return from one furlough, Dr. Chand met us and asked if he could come to our house that evening. Having just had a forty-hour trip that involved travel by taxi, airplane, train, and rickshaw, we were exhausted and in no mood for socializing. But Dr. Chand had just finished his medical training and was leaving for home in Africa the next day. He wanted to talk to me before he left.

After the usual tea, Dr. Chand started to reminisce about his student days. Although not a Christian, he had attended the Friday Groups and learned a lot about the Bible and Christian ethics. He wanted to challenge me.

"Why do you missionaries come here and try to change us? What is so great about Christ?"

I asked him what year it was.

After he answered, I went on to ask him why most of the world dated time from the birth of Christ. We went on to discuss who in history had most influenced the world. He agreed that it was Jesus. Chand also agreed that Jesus was the only perfect person the world had known.

Finally, at four the next morning he left. Dr. Chand did not become a Christian, but it was talks such as this (although better held at earlier hours) that provided opportunities to share our faith.

Many students were changed in other ways by their experiences at Ludhiana. Dr. Ram was an example of this, one that was repeated many times. A staunch Hindu, he had graduated with a good academic record and then taken a residency in internal medicine. He became an excellent physician, and would have joined our faculty had we had an opening. Instead he went to

Where Is God Not?

New Delhi and, at a much better salary, joined one of the largest and most prestigious teaching hospitals. He seemed to be well-settled and to have an excellent future.

Six months later, when I was serving as the medical superintendent of the hospital, he met me in the corridor. He stopped me, and said that he had been looking for me.

"I want a job."

I answered him, "I wish I could help you but we have no vacancies now. We'll keep you in mind if one opens up."

"You owe me a job."

This I could not understand for he had a good job, earning more than twice what we could ever offer him. We owed him nothing. In fact, he was in our debt, for his medical education was partly subsidized and he had received the best training possible. I told him so.

He was not convinced. "You have ruined me."

I asked him what he meant.

"Although the doctors where I work give good enough medical treatment, no one cares about the patients as human beings. You ruined me for working elsewhere."

Fortunately for him, within a few days a vacancy became available in our leprosy program. This he accepted gladly.

We thanked God that we "ruined" many doctors.

CHAPTER 29

Life in a Goldfish Bowl

BISHOP GURBACHAN SINGH ASKED BARBARA, "WOULD YOU be willing to be the manager of Ewing Christian School?"

"I know nothing about running a school."

"Will you think about it?"

"Yes."

It was a rainy evening and I was leading a "journal club," an informal gathering in our home where the surgical staff could meet weekly and discuss articles in medical journals. The lights had just gone out, when there was a knock at the door. Bishop Gurbachan Singh, the Bishop of Chandigarh, and Dr. W. S. Theophilus, the chairman of the Punjab Education Board of the Diocese of Chandigarh, had come to see Barbara. They wanted her to be the manager of one of the sections of the Ewing Christian School. This school had been founded in 1834 by the British Political Officer, Captain John Wade, just before Lowrie's arrival. It was now run by the Church of North India.

In one section, all classes were taught in English. This was what was called an "English Medium School." After much discussion, she did agree and became the manager of the English section. Soon this became an independent school renamed the St. Thomas School.

Where Is God Not?

Barbara served as manager for the next eleven years until we retired. She worked with three principals, was responsible for the finances, paid bills and salaries, helped recruit staff, planned buildings, and supervised their construction. During this time, the enrollment increased from three hundred to over eleven hundred.

During our first years in India, she had taught our children at home, managed our household, and learned the language, the latter far better than I did. Of necessity she became a most reluctant but safe anesthetist.

Soon she was the nursing superintendent of the sanatorium, supervising the work of the nurses, orderlies, and kitchen staff, as well as the purchase and storage of medicines. She acquired such useful knowledge as how much wood to buy for a cremation, and how to find out if the milk had been watered down or otherwise adulterated. Later she turned these responsibilities over to Sister Taj James, a wonderful Indian nurse and close friend.

In Ludhiana, Barbara served as secretary for the surgical department, keeping our records, typing medical papers and scores of theses* for the increasing number of surgical residents. She wrote most of our letters to our friends and churches abroad, although, as she often said, "Forrest signs a good letter."

She also ran the publicity department briefly and then the institutional guest house as well as being involved in the childcare center.

But without doubt the most important contribution she made was providing a Christian home. This soon became a haven for a steady stream of surgical residents who drank thousands of cups of coffee and tea in winter and gallons of cold drinks in summer. At the many hundreds of journal clubs she greeted the young doctors and made them welcome. Her witness was in her living.

Finally, she gave me the loving care and support I needed, often during very dark times and hours.

---

*As part of their training, the Punjab University, like all others in India, required all residents to write a thesis in the subject of their chosen speciality.

The India we left in 1986 was very different from that which had welcomed us thirty-three years earlier. Then it had been independent for less than seven years, was tentative in its administration, and without an industrial base of consequence. The country desperately needed to increase its food production, expand its educational facilities, and improve its medical services. The north was inundated with refugees.

Foreigners were treated deferentially, often being asked to go to the head of queues, and accorded a status they did not merit or necessarily want. We always felt uncomfortable about this. In later years, many of those offering us similar treatment did so because, as they said, they considered us guests of the country, and India is a land rightly famed for its hospitality.

The country developed a vast industrial base, much of it in the Punjab. It went from struggling to cope with a massive influx of refugees from Pakistan to welcoming workers from states to the east and south. Factories sprang up, producing woolen sweaters and socks, sporting goods, bicycles, sewing machines, lathes, and hundreds of other items. Many were for export, going to Europe, Russia, the USA, and elsewhere, providing much-needed foreign exchange.

As we watched, India grew to agricultural maturity and went from being dependent upon foreign aid for its very food to self-sufficiency despite an ever increasing population. Areas of the Punjab around us boasted the highest wheat yield in the world. The government properly had made agriculture its top priority; this, in turn, created the miracle known as the "green revolution." And it was a miracle indeed.

Many factors led to the "green revolution." These included the stimulus provided by the American-aided Punjab Agricultural University (strategically located in Ludhiana), the introduction of high-yielding dwarf varieties of grain, and an adequate supply of water. But most important was the tremendous capacity of the Punjabi farmers for hard work.

Where Is God Not?

On our periodic trips to and from Jubar we witnessed a desert transformed into one of the most fertile and richest farmlands in the world. Where little or nothing had grown, fields changed from dismal browns to bright greens, rich with harvest. We commonly began our trips at four or five in the morning and could see farmers already at work sowing, irrigating, or harvesting their crops. When we returned after dusk they were finally wending their way home.

By the time we retired, 85 percent of the farmland was irrigated and the Punjab was India's richest state as well as its breadbasket, growing over half of the country's grain.

On a national level, development was, for the most part, limited to the plains. The mountain people around Jubar were poor when we arrived, and nearly equally so when we left, for the soil was still poor, water in short supply, and the monsoon as fickle as ever. For them, modernization was a dream for the future.

Development included much-needed improvement in surface transportation. While the British left behind a good railway system, roads were in need of repair and modernization. Parallel efforts were made to improve education and soon new schools and colleges were opening their doors. Universal education was the hope, one not yet fulfilled, particularly in the rural countryside. The government stressed the need to educate girls, and we saw the village school near Jubar go from 117 boys and three girls (the latter all daughters of the sanatorium staff) to near equality.

Counterbalancing this progress, the problem of family planning remained unsolved, with the burgeoning population threatening the future. In the middle 1970s the government had strongly promoted all types of family planning programs, often accompanied by threats and coercion. While their ultimate goals may have been commendable, the methods they used were autocratic and high-handed, ultimately contributing to Mrs. Gandhi's downfall at the polls.

Unfortunately, few companies and businesses offered pension plans. Many workers were enrolled in what was called "provident fund." This fund was mandated by the government and subject to its oversight but run by the employer. This was similar to the American social security in that both employee and employer contributed to it. But there were two major differences, the first being that the workers received their entire share in one lump sum upon retirement, the second that while still employed, they could borrow from the fund. If they did, and many did, they then had less available on retirement. Too often they discovered that they had less of a nest egg than expected and needed. As a result they relied on their sons for security in their old age. With a high infant mortality rate, families wanted at least one or preferably two sons for insurance, adding to the population explosion.

Overshadowing everything, especially in the border state of Punjab, was the possibility of war, particularly with Pakistan. When he was prime minister, Nehru had hoped for twenty-five years of peace, preferring locomotives to tanks, and fertilizer to bullets. That was not to be, and conflicts in 1962 with China and in 1965 and 1971 with Pakistan drained funds better spent on development.

Our own city, Ludhiana, grew rapidly, quadrupling in size. Soon the population numbered well over a million. Unfortunately, much of this was unplanned, and was accompanied by a dispro-portionate growth in its slums. Television antennae sprouted from rooftops, transistor radios blared, and traffic clogged the roads.

Laborers came from afar, risking their lives by riding on the top of the trains to avoid paying. They lived in squalor in slums, sending money home to their families. But they were at least gainfully employed.

The educational system of the Christian Medical College also changed, gradually rising to world standards. New and greater emphasis was placed upon postgraduate and residency training, with hundreds of surgeons, internists, pediatricians and other specialists going forth to serve in mission and other hospitals in India and elsewhere. In my own department of surgery, over a hundred residents completed their training and took their places in the medical community, 85 percent in "developing" countries.

Where Is God Not?

In 1953 two thirds of the teaching staff were foreigners; when we retired at the end of 1986, all but four of the ninety-six faculty were Indian. A calculated plan to nationalize the institution had succeeded.

The hospital grew from what one teacher had called a "small mission hospital" of 250 beds to become a major referral center, tripling in size, with dozens of medical specialists, advanced diagnostic facilities, and therapeutic modalities.

A strong and internationally recognized community health program was started, reaching out to scores of villages around Ludhiana, reducing preventable illness and misery, and, equally important, teaching others how to do the same.

A College of Nursing was built and opened, with new courses offering challenging opportunities for training and service. Similarly new courses in medical technology were added, others expanded and improved.

One result of the college's growing reputation was a sharp increase in the number of applicants to the ever increasing list of courses of study, making selection more competitive. By 1986 only one in fifty or sixty applicants could be admitted to the medical course.

As the years progressed, the incoming students grew taller and taller, the obvious result of the nationwide improvement in nutrition.

In 1953 the financial position was tenuous at best, the institution depending on donations from churches and individuals from abroad just to keep open. As one American colleague phrased it, we lived from crisis to crisis. Gradually, with the introduction of better accounting procedures and a genuine, if involuntary, sacrifice by the staff who were paid less than their worth, fiscal stability was achieved. As the institution received ever decreasing monetary help from abroad, it became essentially self-supporting.

When we went to India in 1953, we went as missionaries. We had shared with our supporters that we had grave doubts as to our qualifications as such for neither of our families had any missionary background, and neither of us had a "call." We were Christians and felt that we wanted to help others. Over the years our commitment grew and when we left India, we were proud to have been missionaries and knew that it was what we had been called to do.

Although we went to India as Christians, we could not, nor did we wish to shake our national heritage. When we were in Jubar, we were the only Americans for miles around. What we did was seen to be what all Americans did. Similarly, when the press reported actions of the American government inimical to India, we were considered responsible. Once, after an announcement of further supply of military equipment to Pakistan, we were accosted at the railway station in Kalka and accused of not wanting to help India. Fortunately, most people distinguished between us as individuals and our government, for which we were often grateful. We often wondered if the bureaucrats in Washington realized or even cared how their actions were interpreted abroad.

Living as a Christian in India was in some ways easier than in the USA, for everybody knew what we stood for, and, in turn, what to expect. In our homeland, our identity was lost. On the other hand, being of a different skin color, we could never escape recognition as a foreigner. We lived in a goldfish bowl. We longed to be able to go shopping or on vacation without being noticed.

After living abroad in a developing country for so many years, returning to our own shores permanently was not easy. We had always suffered from culture shock when going in either direction. Although the culture shock we experienced when going to India was understandable and somewhat lessened by our earlier experiences in China, we were still upset and bothered by the dirt, the hunger, and the poverty. On the six-hour train trip from New Delhi to Ludhiana, the train passed through slums exposing the misery of the poor, and the rude huts and shacks they called home. Stray dogs and cows wandered through the garbage-filled streets. Nearby fields served for toilets.

But what we could never get over was the fatalism and hopelessness of many of the poor. They, too, wanted some of the material benefits that others took for granted. They also knew that they would never live to enjoy them. They could only hope that their children might.

Culture shock on returning to our own country was heightened by the simple contrast in the weight of people. In India only the rich could afford the luxury of overeating. We were unaccustomed to a throwaway society, for in India everything possible was used over and over, and then sold to the *kabari* or junk man. Recycling was routine. As one of our graduates wrote us when he had been in the states but a few days, "Here in America everything is either instant, disposable, or plastic." Materialism in our homeland seemed rampant. Television watching replaced socialization, and a five-day week, something we had never experienced before, provided more leisure time.

But we realized that had we not been lucky enough to live abroad, we, too, would have been no different.

But we had, and thank God for it.

Mission Accomplished

THE BOEING 747 DESCENDED GENTLY ONTO THE TARMAC of the Indira Gandhi airport. A little over eight years had passed since we had left India wondering if we would ever return. We were going back to join in the final centennial celebrations of the medical college.

The enervating heat assailed us as we descended the steps of the plane. It was midmorning early in March 1995 and we had forgotten how hot it would be.

Dr. Sumedha Taneja, an old friend and the first woman in our surgical training program, welcomed us warmly. Collecting our luggage, we piled into her tiny car for the ride into New Delhi. We could hardly breathe—the air was more polluted than ever by the exhaust of thousands of trucks and cars and by smoke belching from factories, new and old. Crossing the Jumna (Yamuna) river, we could smell the stench from human waste and other pollutants. If there were other rivers as filthy, we could not name them.

The twin cities of Delhi and New Delhi had grown and the population now numbered nine million. Nearly a third of them lived in slums that we would soon visit.

We spent two days in Delhi, meeting former students and friends. An embarrassed Barbara was quickly whisked off by

Where Is God Not?

Sumedha and Meera, another former surgical resident, to go shopping for a new salwar and kameez. In London she had changed into the one she had worn when we had left India, but Sumedha and Meera said that they were hopelessly out of date and would not let her wear them. That evening we dined with old students and stuffed ourselves with chicken curry and other delights that we had nearly forgotten.

The next morning Dr. Beverly Booth, a fellow Presbyterian missionary, took us to visit some of the slums where she was working.

Like other third-world slums, they beggared description. Located on any available land—by railway tracks, next to sewage canals, or on the banks of the polluted river, the poor lived in tiny eight-by-ten foot shacks made of old kerosene cans, cardboard, plastic sheets, or tar paper. A few of the longtime residents managed to scavenge a few used bricks or discarded sheets of corrugated metal to improve their hovels. Rarely more that five to six feet high inside, adults had to stoop to enter. Windows were a luxury and air stagnated. Women cooked their meager meals outside and everybody slept out-of-doors in the stifling summer heat. In some slums nearly six hundred people shared a single water tap. Sanitation was limited, and thousands used the fields while children squatted over open drains.

Beverly was working with the Emmanuel Hospital Association, an indigenous organization with which I was familiar. They were helping the people to help themselves, to install more water taps, improve sanitation, build medical clinics, and start literacy programs. There was hope.

Shortly before seven next morning we boarded the train for the 190-mile trip to Ludhiana. As we sped through the familiar countryside, it seemed not to have changed greatly—fields had been planted, and farmers were tending their crops as usual. However, the towns and cities along the way had grown, and spread out along the railway line. Congestion was greater than ever.

Many old friends met us at Ludhiana. Among them was Dr. Richard Daniel, a former student and professor of ophthalmology, recently appointed as the director of the institution.

158

Driving through the city, we recalled that this was part of the Grand Trunk Road, immortalized by Kipling. It was also a portion of the route we had walked many years earlier one Christmas Eve when all the Christians in the city marched from the tiny church* in the bazaar to Kalvari Church. As we had paraded through the streets that night long past, shopkeepers of all faiths had joined in the celebration, walking several blocks along with us.

But on this day it was the Sikhs who were celebrating. Hundreds of them marched behind bands in colorful array. We never learned what the occasion was.

As we drove through the gates of the residential compound, we passed the houses we had called home for thirty-two years. We saw the hidden places where our children had played; the gardens we called our own but which really belonged to mali; the trees and bushes we had lovingly planted, now grown to maturity. We remembered the huge red cockroaches in the kitchens Barbara had fought valiantly, but in vain; the time she found a snakeskin on a window sill just before a reporter from *Readers Digest* was to spend the night (he elected to stay elsewhere when he learned about it). We recalled the scores of eager young doctors who had been made welcome in our homes; of the celebrations they held at our house when they passed examinations; of the joy they brought us.

Ludhiana had grown and changed. Increasing prosperity produced an alarming growth in traffic. Merely crossing the street to the hospital challenged one's agility and threatened one's life.

As part of the centennial celebrations, the surgical department had organized a surgical conference in our honor. Most of the speakers were former residents, others were still in training. Clearly the department was progressing and new and more advanced procedures were being done every day. Operations that I had only dreamed of were now routine.

Our students had outstripped their teachers—which was as it should be.

---

*This was the first church in Asia founded by the Presbyterians.

Where Is God Not?

The annual convocation was held as usual on March 24, the birthday of Dr. Edith Brown, the founder of the Christian Medical College.

The day was hotter than usual as the faculty processed in and took their places. Barbara had watched this every year, whereas I was a spectator for the first time. I was no longer on the staff. Seated on the dais were the convocation speaker, the chairman of the board of governors, and the six academic administrators of the institution.

It suddenly dawned on us that for the first time in the history of the institution there were no foreigners on the staff and that all six of the administrators were our graduates. All but the nursing superintendent had been my students.

Exactly one hundred years after its humble beginnings this great institution was finally in the hands of its own graduates. We were grateful to have been a small part of it.

> "We cannot cure all,
> We cannot bring relief to all,
> But we can always care for all."
>
> —*Source unknown*